D. A. KOSTER

Ocean Salvage

D. A. KOSTER

Ocean Salvage

WITH MAPS AND 33 PHOTOGRAPHS

GERALD DUCKWORTH & CO. LTD.
3 HENRIETTA ST. LONDON, W.C.2

First published in 1971

© *1971 by D. A. Koster*

ISBN 0 7156 0561 5

PRINTED IN GREAT BRITAIN
BY EBENEZER BAYLIS & SON LIMITED
THE TRINITY PRESS, WORCESTER, AND LONDON

CONTENTS

LIST OF ILLUSTRATIONS

ACKNOWLEDGMENTS

1*a*, 2*a*, 2*b*, 9*b*: Ditta Roberto Galeazzi S. p. A.

1*b*, 4*a*, 4*c*, 4*d*: Andrew Pope

3*a*, 3*b*: Imperial College, London, and Enfield College of
Technology, Malta Expedition, 1969

5*a*, 5*b*: Kelvin Hughes

6: Cunard Steamship Company

7*a*, 8*b*: George G. Harrap & Company from *The Man who
Bought a Navy* by Gerald Bowman

7*b*, 8*a*: Siebe Gorman & Company from *Deep Diving and
Submarine Operations* by Robert H. Davis

9*a*, 9*c*: S. P. A. Sandberg

10*a*: Union Steamship Company of New Zealand

10*b*, 11*a*: *Sydney Morning Herald* (London Representatives)

11*b*: New Zealand Newspapers Limited

12: H.M. Stationery Office, London

13*a*: Royal Navy Official Photo, Crown Copyright. Courtesy
of the Ministry of Defence (DNSY).

13*b*, 14*a*, 14*b*, 15*a*, 15*b*, 16*a*, 16*b*: Official U.S. Navy Photographs

PREFACE

My thanks are due to all those included in the list of acknowledgments for the valuable assistance which I have received
from them; without it much of the book could never have been
written.

I should like to mention particularly Commander Joseph
W. Marshall, the Chief of the Magazine and Book Division of
the Directorate of Defense Information in Washington who has
been extremely helpful in providing me with the material
which made it possible to include the *Thresher, Scorpion* and
Palomares incidents.

In addition to the listed acknowledgments, I am most
grateful for the help I have received from my own family during
the actual writing of the book, and from my brother and his
wife, Mr. and Mrs. R. V. Koster who read the whole script
over and offered much advice.

D.A.K.

New Milton, Hampshire.
May, 1970

ACKNOWLEDGMENTS

Admiralty Research Laboratory, Teddington, Middlesex;
Bank of England, London, E.C.2; Board of Trade, Marine
Division, London, E.C.1; British Overseas Airways Corpora-
tion, London, S.W.1; Captain Lewis B. Melson, USN (Retd.),
La Mesa, California, U.S.A.; Cunard Line Limited, London,
S.W.1; Directorate for Defense Information, Office of Assistant
Secretary of Defense, Washington, D.C., U.S.A.; Ditta
Roberto Galeazzi, S.p.A., La Spezia, Italy; Her Majesty's
Stationery Office, London, E.C.1; Hydrographic Department,

ACKNOWLEDGMENTS

Ministry of Defence, Taunton, Somerset; Imperial College of Science and Technology, London, S.W.7; John Fairfax & Sons (Australia) Limited, London, E.C.4; Kelvin Hughes, London, E.C.3; Messrs. Sandberg, Consulting, Inspecting and Testing Engineers, London, S.W.1; Ministry of Defence, Navy Office, Wellington, New Zealand; Andrew Pope, Warsash, Southampton; Don Jones, Penarth, Cardiff; S. P. A. Sandberg, Washington, Nr. Worthing, Sussex; National Maritime Museum, Greenwich, London, S.E.10; New Zealand High Commission, London, S.W.1; New Zealand Newspapers Limited, Auckland, New Zealand; Peninsular and Oriental Steam Navigation Company, London, E.C.3; Public Affairs Office, C-in-C, United States Naval Forces, Europe, London, W.1; Public Affairs Office, U.S. Naval Ordnance Test Station, Pasadena, California, U.S.A.; Pye TVT Limited, Cambridge; Salvage Association, London, E.C.3; Siebe Gorman & Company Limited, Chessington, Surrey; Sir John Williams, The Australian National Line, Melbourne, Australia; The *Auckland Star*, Auckland, New Zealand; The Decca Navigator Company Limited, London, S.E.1; The Duke of Argyll; The Marconi Company Limited, Chelmsford, Essex; The New Zealand Shipping Company Limited, London, E.C.3; The Northern Publishing Company Limited, Whangarei, New Zealand; Union Steam Ship Company of New Zealand Limited, Wellington, New Zealand; United States Naval Institute, Annapolis, Maryland, U.S.A.

Two chapters from this book have appeared in *Blackwood's Magazine*—chapter 11 under the title 'Jigsaw Puzzle' in August 1968, and chapter 14 in March 1971—and I am grateful for the editor's kind permission to include them here.

PART ONE

CHAPTER ONE

HISTORY

The planet Earth on which we live is thought to be between four and five thousand million years old.

The exact date of its birth is not, of course, recorded at Somerset House, or anywhere else for that matter, if for no other reason than that the stupendous event, as well as having occurred, possibly, several hundred million or even a thousand million years earlier or later, was itself spread over an enormous period in time.

What is, however, certain is that nobody was there to witness its creation, and it does not matter very much that the actual date—if one can refer to this place in time as a 'date'—is somewhat obscure, although the earth's crust is now believed to have formed about four thousand five hundred million years ago. Of much greater interest is the fact that some sort of microscopic life appeared about three thousand seven hundred million years later and that seaweeds and invertebrates seem to have made a fairly 'sudden' appearance on the sea floor about two hundred million years after that. Life, in those far distant days, six hundred million years back in time, was entirely water-borne and only succeeded in crawling out of the sea and establishing itself on dry land some two hundred and fifty million years ago when the first amphibians evolved.

Mammals appeared on the scene about one hundred and fifty million years later, but it was another hundred and ninety nine million years or so before the primordial ape finally

I

descended from the trees, acquired the ability to walk upright on the ground and took on the likeness of man. This, the advent of man, happened about seven hundred thousand years ago which is only 'yesterday' by comparison with other dates in the earth's time-table.

It is an interesting thought that life, having taken that fantastic period in time, four hundred and fifty million years, to rid itself of the necessity to live in the sea should, so soon, commence the struggle in reverse and seek ways and means of returning to it. But hundreds of millions of years—even just millions, like millions of miles or millions of pounds—are quite beyond the scope of the ordinary person's imagination. Such periods of time, such distances or sums of money mean little until they are reduced to more understandable proportions.

A man's life span is, however, within the bounds of his understanding and so, if we take someone born in 1900 and now aged 70 or thereabouts, and his life as representing the whole life span of man himself, 700,000 years, then that almost pre-historic record of a naked diver going down to 50 feet in the Mediterranean in the year 3,300 B.C. would have occurred only just over 27 weeks ago. During the last three months, man would have invented diving dresses and submarines, landed on the moon, and reached, in a bathyscaph, a record depth of 35,802 feet—equal to a land distance of nearly 7 miles.

On the same time scale, the first mammals would have evolved about 18,000 B.C. The first amphibians would have emerged from the sea about 33,000 B.C.—but already our time scale, which would put the Battle of Hastings just over a month ago and the Second World War less than 22 hours ago, becomes quite useless.

The art of diving has been practised ever since primitive man used shell fish for food and pearls and corals were adapted for personal ornament. But the longest time a good diver can remain underwater without artificial means is about three minutes and so, from the very earliest times, man has sought to perfect instruments which would enable him to stay down for longer periods.

So, by a little over 5,000 years ago, he had already acquired the ability to get back into the water, to reach down again

2

beneath the surface of the sea, if only for very brief periods. In ancient Greek and Roman records there are references to men diving for oysters, pearls, coral and sponges, and the historian Herodotus writing about 450 B.C., tells how a diver named Scyllias wrecked one of Xerxes' galleys by cutting her moorings underwater. A few years later Thucydides (about 465–400 B.C.) described how some divers, during the siege of Syracuse in Sicily in 415–413 B.C., sawed away underwater barriers. And during the siege of Tyre in 332 B.C. Alexander the Great ordered divers to destroy undersea defences.

Man's inventive genius was growing apace. Aristotle, who lived between 384 and 322 B.C., wrote that divers were using devices to enable them to stay down longer and said that some breathed underwater by letting down a metallic vessel which retained air within it.

Now, if an empty glass tumbler is turned upside down and pushed downwards into a bowl of water, the air inside becomes compressed upwards in direct proportion to the depth at which it is held, the air pressure being balanced by that of the water at its own level inside the mouth of the container. Fix a heavy iron ring to the mouth of the tumbler so that it sinks under its own weight and you have a miniature diving bell. If the weighted tumbler is then lowered to a depth of 33 feet, where the pressure of water is double atmospheric pressure at sea level, the volume of air inside is reduced by half. If, then, by means of a tube, more air is forced into the tumbler so that the pressure of the air inside is raised to slightly above that existing at the depth of the container, the level of the water inside will drop until the air begins to spill out and escape from around the rim.

Had man, therefore, over 2,200 years ago, in his struggle to return under water, already invented the diving bell?

Aristotle also recorded that Alexander the Great himself descended in a 'diving machine' which he called Colimpha. It must have had some sort of windows, for it is reported to have let in the light, and it also enabled the man inside to keep dry. Was this, then, the first observation chamber?

Man was truly on his way back to the sea long before he looked up and saw, low over Bethlehem, the bright star which was to herald in the birth of the Christian era.

But diving, as a business, and without any kind of breathing aid, has been carried on by naked pearl fishers in the Persian Gulf since the time of the Macedonians in the fourth century B.C., as well as in the ancient fisheries of the Gulf of Mannar, on the west side of Ceylon and in the Tinnevelly fishery in the strait between the Isle of Mannar and the mainland. In the Persian Gulf, several hundred Arab dhows still carry out pearl fishing and use methods which have changed little through the centuries.

The diver, wearing nothing more than a loin cloth and a nose clip, but with fingers and big toes protected by leather sheaths, goes down with a string bag slung round his neck. A large stone is attached to the end of a rope which has a loop in it, just above the stone, into which the diver puts his foot and he is then lowered on to the sea bed. A second and smaller rope is tied to the string bag and is used for hauling it to the surface as soon as the man below has filled it with oysters.

These divers usually work in depths of between 60 and 90 feet and stay down for as long as a minute and a half. In the course of a day's work, each diver makes about thirty descents, after which he is utterly exhausted. His working life, too, is brief compared with that of other professions. These pearl divers are, generally, short-lived men and the price of pearls should be measured in lives as well as in money.

In the Indian waters, boats operate in groups of sixty or seventy. Each boat carries ten divers who work in pairs and take it in turns to dive. One man goes down on a stone-weighted rope, like his Arab counterpart, but carries a basket, instead of a bag, for his oysters. He takes down with him, attached to his basket, a small line by which he signals to the other man in the boat when to haul up the basket. Here the average diver remains down for between 50 and 80 seconds, though cases are known of these men remaining submerged for as long as 6 minutes—an incredible length of time to an ordinary person, whose limit for keeping his head under water is usually nearer 6 seconds.

The depth to which some of these naked divers can descend also staggers the imagination and there is on record the case of a

4

Greek diver, Stotti Georghios, who in 1913, in the Adriatic, reached a depth of 200 feet.

Until the thirteenth century, no great strides seem to have been made towards developing mechanical aids to the human lung in prolonging man's stay under water. Roger Bacon, in 1240, mentioned instruments which would enable a man to walk on the sea bed and later, about the year 1500, Leonardo da Vinci designed several varieties of diving appliance, some of which incorporated a floating air pipe. In 1679 C. A. Borelli described a device which consisted of a leather bottle containing air which would be carried on the diver's back and operated by a piston, but it seems that this contraption could not have been very successful, and it died a natural death.

Rudimentary forms of appliance to enable a man to breathe under water were introduced into England towards the end of the seventeenth century and a primitive conception of diving dress and observation chamber combined was produced by John Lethbridge of Devon in 1715. His apparatus consisted of a leather barrel, with an observation porthole; from the barrel protruded two sleeves for the man's arms. It could not be used in depths of more than 10 feet—but it was a definite beginning. After all, the first aeroplane did not, initially, get as far as that off the ground.

The earliest forms of diving bell had to be brought to the surface for a fresh supply of air, but about 1780 Sir Edmund Halley (of Halley's comet fame) contrived means of renewing the air in a diving bell by using barrels filled with air. These had holes in the bottom and were lowered to the required depth. The bell, in this case, was a truncated wooden cone and Dr. Halley claimed that, by conveying fresh air to his diving bell in this way, it was possible for a man to remain at a depth of 60 feet for up to one and a half hours at a time.

Nearly 80 years later, in 1797, K. H. Klingert of Breslau designed and produced a diving suit consisting of a leather jacket and drawers which were to be used in conjunction with an egg-ended metallic cylinder. The garments had tight-fitting arms and legs. The diver, attired in this sort of medieval leather armour, was then 'fitted' into the cylinder which completely enveloped his head and body down to the hips. The egg-ended

5

top fitted over his head and air was supplied from a container by means of a pipe with an ivory mouthpiece. Going home at night, in his working clothes, Klingert's diver must have been a grotesque sight.

But man, in his efforts to perfect the means of working under water, was on the right road at last. An important advance was made in 1802 by William Forder who used bellows to maintain the air pressure inside the diver's dress at that of the water outside, which prevented the dress from collapsing under the pressure and so suffocating the diver.

In 1819, the great Siebe Gorman invented his open diving dress. It was far from perfect as nothing but the air pressure inside the metal helmet, which was attached to a waterproof leather jacket, kept the level of the water inside below the diver's chin and thus prevented him from drowning. Air was supplied by a pressure pump, through a flexible tube connected to the helmet, and the diver had to remain upright. But it was the real beginning, and after a great many experiments the year 1830 saw the introduction of the closed diving dress, the principles of which have remained in universal use to this day, although numerous notable improvements have been made since Siebe Gorman's death in 1872.

Modern diving dress consists of seven main parts: the waterproof dress itself, an incompressible metal helmet with breastplate, a pair of 16 lb. weighted boots, two 40 lb. breast and back plates and a flexible, non-compressible air tube—non-compressible because a much greater quantity of air must be supplied the deeper a diver descends.

In pearl and other skin diving, where no equipment is used, before leaving the surface the diver has to fill his lungs completely and compress the air taken in as much as possible, so as to maintain the balance between internal and external pressures. Then, as he goes down, the increase in water pressure reduces the lung volume until he reaches a depth where the condition of his lungs is similar to that on the surface after total exhalation.

Water pressure increases at the rate of 0·444 lb. per square inch for each foot of depth or, in other words, the equivalent of atmospheric pressure, 14·7 lb. per square inch, for each 33

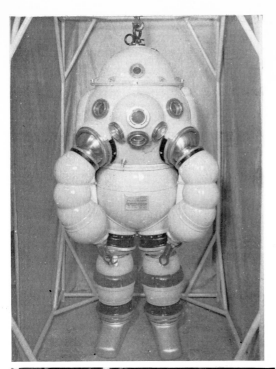

Plate 1 *a* and *b*,
Articulated metal
diving dress by
Roberto Galeazzi

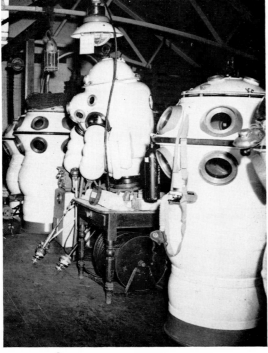

Plate 2a and b,
Butoscopic turret
by Roberto Galeazzi

feet of depth. Because of this, a diver on the surface requires about 1·5 cubic feet of air per minute; at 33 feet, where the pressure per square inch outside the tube, and also on the diver's suit, is double that on the surface, he must be supplied with three cubic feet a minute. At 99 feet, where it is 44 lb. per square inch above surface atmospheric pressure, he requires six cubic feet a minute and at double that depth, at 198 feet, where the water pressure is 88 lb. per square inch, 10·5 cubic feet a minute.

After 1872, experiments were made with a form of rigid metal diving dress or, more appropriately, diving armour. An early example, the design of which followed, the shape of the human body, was produced in 1875 by a Frenchman named Lafayette. About three years later the French brothers Carmagnolle designed a complete suit of heavy armour incorporating mechanical joints, and actually produced one in 1882.

In contrast to the soft diving dress, where the diver breathes air under pressure which increases with the depth, the rigid metal suit allowed him to breathe air at very nearly atmospheric pressure, whatever the depth. British designers, however, appeared to have turned away from this line of development and in 1913 the German firm of Neufeldt & Kuhnke of Kiel, working on an invention of a German schoolmaster, began designing an articulated metal diving shell.

The first version was produced in 1920. It was made in two portions bolted together at the waist, with three flexible arm joints on ball bearings, at shoulder, elbow and wrists, and two in each leg, at thigh and ankle. The helmet was surmounted by a large flotation ring, a form of ballast tank, which could be flooded at will and emptied by 'blowing' with compressed air from an attached cylinder. The CO_2 content of the exhaled air was absorbed by a regenerator and a fresh supply of oxygen was available from a row of oxygen bottles carried on the back, but these were unprotected and liable to accidental damage. In 1923 this diving shell was tested with great success in a deep water lake in the Tyrol.

A second version, lighter and simpler in construction, had a smooth dome-shaped top and the oxygen bottles were more protected. A team of German divers actually used this model in an endeavour to establish communication with the sunken British submarine M.1 off Portland in 1925.

Having found that man, encased in a shell of metal armour which could withstand enormous pressures, and breathing re-oxygenated air at very little above normal atmospheric pressure, could descend to hitherto unthought-of depths, attention turned to the possibilities of constructing apparatus in which a man could move about freely and not be restricted by a metal diving suit conforming to the shape of the human body.

The diving bell permitted this freedom up to a point, and rudimentary forms of the bell had been experimented with since antiquity. But the depth to which it could be used was limited because of the pressure of the air inside, which, even at 33 feet, is double that on the surface, and the air contained in the bell had to be renewed in order to provide the diver with sufficient oxygen.

Air is a mechnical mixture of 21 per cent volume of oxygen, 78 per cent volume of nitrogen and 1 per cent of other gases. If a lighted candle is fixed to a floating cork on water and pressed down by placing a tumbler over it, the flame will be extinguished as soon as the oxygen content of the air inside is exhausted. So, under the same conditions, would a man die.

Oxygen bottles, therefore, had to be included in all forms of deep diving apparatus.

More recently, a steel diving 'bell' by the firm of Siebe Gorman was used in the construction of Dover harbour. It was 17 feet long, 10½ feet wide and 7 feet high, fitted with electric lighting and a telephone, and could be used at a maximum depth of 60 feet. Air was supplied by a steam-driven compressor, and a steel shaft incorporating two airtight doors with an 8 foot airlock between provided access from the surface to the steel working chamber.

But the armoured diving dress was to be the subject of still further development and was finding favour with at least one of the designers of diving apparel, the firm of Roberto Galeazzi of Spezia, Italy, who produced a simplified form of the Neufeldt & Kuhnke dress. The joints were reduced to six, two in each leg and one at each shoulder. The body was a one-piece shell surrounded by a ring-shaped ballast tank, and the very large

helmet was closed by a simple cover plate. It was roomy and
the diver could extract his arms from the sleeves and do work
inside. The air supply was again self-contained and sufficient
for six hours continuous diving, the shell being designed to withstand the pressure at a depth of 700 feet, equal to 20 atmospheres.
(Plate 1a and b.)

Science fiction writers, wondering how they should depict
their men from Mars, would not have lacked ideas if they had
studied the Klingert fashion magazine of 1797, or 'What's New
in Swim Wear' by Neufeldt & Kuhnke in the 1920s.

Another Italian firm, the Societa Recuperi Marittimi,
known as SORIMA, obtained the right to use of the Neufeldt
& Kuhnke diving shell in Italian waters and successfully used
it in salvage operations in the Mediterranean in 1926. This type
of diving shell was also carried by the salvage vessel *Artiglio*
which succeeded in recovering the gold from the wreck of the
liner *Egypt* in the early 1930s. These shells were made of cast
steel in one piece, open at the top which was covered by a
detachable circular lid. This improved type weighed 800 lb. in
air but only about 40 lb. when submerged with the ballast tank
filled, and had the same six flexible joints; but the arms ter-
minated in steel pincers on small ball-bearing joints to enable
the diver to pick up objects. The arms could still be withdrawn
from the hollow sleeves of the shell and the diver had telephone
communication with the surface vessel. (Plate 9b.) He breathed
the same air and wore a respirator connected to a canister
containing chemicals to absorb the carbon dioxide, and one
canister enabled him to stay below for three hours. Spare
canisters were carried when required for longer periods under
water. The shell had a large glass window in front and a smaller
one at each side and overhead, and it was designed for safe use
at a depth of 600 feet.

When John Lethbridge, in 1715, produced his leather
barrel with two sleeves for the diver's arms and an observation
porthole for him to see through he had, in fact, though without
knowing it, invented something which had the rudiments of
both diving armour and observation chamber.

The articulated diving armour solved the problem of pressure; the chemical canister and oxygen bottle made the diver

9

independent of a piped air supply and the under-water telephone did away with the necessity for him to signal to the surface by means of a cord.

But a diver is required to do various jobs under water and, above all, to be able to pick up things on the bottom or from a wreck. The steel pincers had replaced the diver's hands but, as he could now talk to those on the vessel above, why not larger pincers, as a separate piece of equipment, and operated from above under directions from the diver?

Then why restrict the diver to a suit of metal armour? Put him into a cylindrical metal container with portholes and exterior lighting and let him see to place a large grab, operated by the salvage vessel above, which could bite out and pick up tons at a time—and the recovery of treasure from hundreds of feet down would no longer be just a dream. It would, and did, become a reality.

So came the observation chamber—based on a principle designed by R. H. Davies over 30 years previously and incorporating the under-water telephone invented by Siebe Gorman more than half a century ago—a version of which, produced by Roberto Galeazzi, was extensively used by SORIMA on the *Egypt* salvage operations.

The larger of Roberto Galeazzi's present production models, which they call a Butoscopic Turret, is over six and a half feet high, has a maximum diameter of almost four feet, weighs nearly two and a half tons with detachable ballast weights and is designed for use in depths of up to 1,800 feet. It has eighteen windows and the diver's seat is supported on a rotating frame, which enable him to see in any direction without effort. (Plates 2a and b.)

Exterior lighting, controlled by the diver, is provided by three 1,000-watt lamps powered either by accumulators or as a separate plant with electricity supply from the surface vessel. The accumulators can provide over four hours lighting with one lamp, or nearly one hour when using all three lamps. Accessories include a luminous depth gauge, a barometer for atmospheric pressure control, two collapsible writing tables, oxygen bottles and chemical canisters. Truly a one-man under-water operations room with every modern convenience.

As in all other spheres of exploration, man's inventive genius increased his ability to go farther, higher, faster and deeper. The observation chamber could take him down to 1,800 feet but the deepest sea could, by comparison, cover the top of the loftiest mountain in the world by more than a mile and so provided the greater challenge. The highest mountain was no longer an unconquered goal, but no man yet knew what the deepest ocean might reveal and his insatiable curiosity stirred him to even greater efforts to explore the unknown depths

So to the Bathysphere, designed by the New York zoologist Dr. William Beebe in 1934. It was a spherical steel casting, one and a half inches thick, four feet nine inches in diameter and weighed 5,000 lb. In this steel ball, fitted with observaton windows, Dr. Beebe descended 3,028 feet off south-east Bermuda. But even this great depth was to be made to seem no more, relatively, than a dive into a swimming bath.

Auguste Piccard was born in 1884 and, fourteen years after Dr. Beebe's historic descent in 1934, Piccard succeeded in producing what he called a Bathyscaph. He was financed by the Fonds National de la Recherche Scientifique Belge and his first invention was only a kind of balloon, but his second, called FNRS 2, was completed in 1948. It was designed to resist a pressure of 5,700 lb. per square inch, equal to that at a depth of 13,000 feet, but was found to be insufficiently strong to withstand the action of rough seas on the surface. Nevertheless it actually made an unmanned descent to 3,600 feet.

A second Bathyscaph design, FNRS 3, constructed at Toulon, made a manned descent in the Atlantic in February 1954 and reached a depth of 13,287 feet—a stupendous advance.

Auguste Piccard's son, Dr. Jacques Piccard, continued the work his father had so successfully begun. With the assistance of the Italian Navy, which had collaborated in the production of FNRS 2, a third and larger Bathyscaph called the *Trieste* was built. This was, basically, a steel sphere surmounted by a steel entrance shaft or conning tower 18 feet high. Without additional buoyancy it would have sunk like a stone and while this was, in effect, what was required, its sinking had to be controlled and it had to be able to come up again, and both of these functions were made possible by a unique adaptation. It made use of tanks filled with petrol, which is lighter than water, and this enabled the *Trieste*, in the first instance, to float on the surface. The petrol tanks were fitted on either side of the passenger sphere. Extra air chambers at both ends, beyond the petrol tanks, provided additional buoyancy during towing and also gave the Bathyscaph its submarine-like shape.

When the air chambers were filled with water the craft commenced submerging. The petrol tanks, divided into compartments, were designed to allow controlled entry of sea water. As the craft descended and water entered the tanks, the petrol became compressed and pressure inside and out was equalized, so the Bathyscaph continued to sink. The cold sea water also made the petrol contract by cooling, and some of it could also be released if required to give added weight to the vessel.

To make the Bathyscaph rise, water was blown out of the petrol compartments and the petrol thereby increased its own volume, thus providing more buoyancy. Additional control, either in slowing its descent or making it rise faster, was provided by ballast consisting of four and a half tons of small iron shot which was carried in two bins, one on either side of the sphere. The balls of shot were held in their containers by magnetism and they could be released at will, and in any quantity, by cutting off the electric current from the coils surrounding the openings of the bins.

On January 23rd, 1960, after previously completing as many as sixty-nine successful dives, the *Trieste* with three men aboard, prepared for its seventieth and deepest descent—to the bottom of the Marianas Trench in the Pacific, the greatest known ocean depth in the world.

They began to submerge just after eight o'clock in the morning, slowly at first because everything was being tested to ensure a successful dive, and for the first half hour their speed of descent was limited to about 20 feet per minute. All went well as they passed the 650 feet mark and increased their rate of sinking. In less than an hour after leaving the surface they were down to 2,000 feet and then, in absolute darkness, continued dropping to 26,000 feet at which point their controlled descent was slowed to two feet per second, a rate which was further reduced to one foot per second when 30,000 feet was reached. They were now a thousand feet deeper than Mount Everest is high, and more than fifteen times deeper than man had ever been before.

In 1875, the greatest depth found in the Marianas Trench by HMS *Challenger*, the Admiralty survey ship, had been 26,850 feet, but this was by the old-fashioned method of letting down a wire with a lead weight on the end until it touched bottom. Over 80 years later, during the International Geophysical Year of 1957–58, the Russian survey ship *Vityaz* recorded a depth of 36,056 feet, the greatest so far known.

But now, before the descent of the *Trieste*, the attendant USS *Lewis* and her destroyer escort had tried to find the deepest part of Marianas Trench by exploding TNT on the sea bed and measuring the time taken for the sound waves to reach the surface. By this method—which is not altogether reliable at great depths because of the unknown degree of salinity and temperature, both of which affect the speed of sound in water—they found a place 33,600 feet deep and here the *Trieste* had dived.

At 33,000 feet, however, with the expected bottom a mere 600 feet below them, nothing which even faintly resembled sea bed appeared on their depth recorder. Slowly, warily, they went deeper. At 34,000 feet, when they were 400 feet below where they should have touched bottom there was still nothing. Their thoughts, then, can only be imagined. Dare they go deeper? If their steel monster continued to function would they just go on, sinking deeper and deeper, only to find—nothing. Nothing but a deep and bottomless pit—a watery grave, in complete and utter darkness and loneliness—and then, if something went wrong, a loneliness and darkness from which they would never return. They must have felt a long, long way from home at that moment.

Deeper yet—and at 35,000 feet they saw on their depth-recorder the first signs of the sea bed beneath them. Just after one o'clock, five hours after leaving the blessed sunshine above, the Bathyscaph came gently to rest on the smooth off-white ooze of the bottom of the Marianas Trench. They had descended to a record depth of 35,800 feet.

Just expressing it in figures like that does not really convey what such a depth really means in terms of going down. If it were possible to construct an ordinary ladder long enough to reach to the surface from the bottom of the Marianas Trench, and one went down that ladder at the rate of one rung per second, it would take over thirteen hours' uninterrupted descent to reach the sea bed. But, of course, it would be quite impossible for anyone ever to do that, for many reasons. For one thing, the pressure down there is in the region of seven tons per square inch, which is more than 1,000 times greater than the pressure under which we live on the earth's surface—and no human body could withstand that.

The *Trieste*, on this occasion commanded by Lieutenant Don Walsh of the US Navy and with Dr. Jacques Piccard and Guiseppe Buono, her master mechanic, on board, stayed on the bottom for about twenty minutes before releasing ballast and beginning the ascent. At first they rose at only one foot per second, but as the petrol expanded owing to the decreasing pressure outside, this rate speeded up to a maximum of four feet per second, reducing again as the warmer water near the surface increased the Bathyscaph's 'apparent' weight. Just under three and a half hours after leaving the bottom it was floating on the surface once more—and their historic, record-making dive was over.

Less than 10 years later, a team of young British scientists and engineers from the Imperial and Enfield Colleges of Science and Technology designed and built an inflatable under-water house and moored it thirty feet down in seventy feet of water in Paradise Bay, Malta. This cottage-loaf shaped house weighed only 400 lb. in air. It was 9 feet long, 7 feet high, 6 feet wide and equipped with lighting, telephone, and small immersion heaters for their domestic fresh water. In this house—which marine estate agents of the future would surely describe as 'Mst. dsrble. mini-res. ev. mod. con. h&c. tel.'—five members of the team lived and worked in pairs for periods of up to four days, (Plates 3a and b.)

Air inside the house was kept breathable by a battery-operated 'life support module' and all occupants were able to keep dry and sleep comfortably at night. During this most successful trial of the submarine residence a telephone call was actually made direct from the under-water house to England.

Perhaps we have already started on the long road back to a completely watery environment, though man's amazing achievements in reaching out into space seem to indicate that his major efforts are being made in this latter direction—up rather than down.

CHAPTER TWO

SALVAGE OPERATIONS

Ever since man first went down to the sea in ships, ships too have gone down, for a variety of reasons. In the earliest days most of the wrecks were probably, caused by weather or by lack of knowledge of what lay beneath the surface of an apparently safe expanse of water. A violent gale blowing over hundreds of miles of open water can produce waves 40 feet in height, measured from trough to crest, but even these would not break on rocks more than 40 feet below the surface. In any case, in such conditions the whole surface of the sea is white with breaking crests, and shoal patches are difficult to detect. Similarly, in moderately rough weather, such as primitive vessels might be expected to venture out in, with waves up to 10 feet high for instance, rocks deeper than 10 feet would produce no additional surface disturbance and so pass unnoted.

Today, most areas used by shipping have been adequately surveyed and charted, but it is economically impossible to explore every square yard, or even every square mile, of the ocean bed and even now there are areas hundreds of square miles in extent which are assumed to be free of dangerous rocks only by reason of the general depths and contours of the surrounding areas.

Take, for instance, a shipping route one mile wide across the narrowest part of the English Channel, from Dover to

Calais. Such an area could be depicted on a large scale chart of six inches to one mile, and measuring 42 inches by 18 inches, in three sections of seven miles each.

The greatest number of soundings which can be legibly shown on one square inch of a chart is 100, and if one set out to survey the 21 square miles of sea bed so as to show this density of soundings, no fewer than 75,000 separate depth recordings would have to be taken. More than adequate, one might think, to ensure that no dangerous rocks or shoals would be missed. Yet hazards as large as a tennis court, or rocks the size of a large house, could easily be left undetected, for each sounding would record the depth at only one spot in each 100-foot square patch of sea bed.

Even by using a modern depth-recorder, which takes a continuous line of soundings, there would still be 100-foot square patches of unsounded ocean floor between the lines. On a scale of one inch to one mile each sounding would represent an area of more than 41,000 square yards equivalent to over eight acres of ground.

Small wonder, then, that ships were—and occasionally still are—wrecked on uncharted reefs, and no wonder at all when there were no charts to guide them.

If a ship sinks in deep water it is no hazard to other vessels sailing over it, and of no further interest to man, except when the nature and value of its cargo makes salvage profitable.

Refloating a wrecked ship is rarely simple, usually difficult, and sometimes impossible. Unless it lies in the entrance to a harbour or is otherwise a hindrance or a danger to other shipping, or if it has little value as scrap, or contains a cargo so ruined by sea water that it also is valueless, then no effort is made to salvage it, and it is left for time and tide to complete its destruction. Its only immortality, should it have sunk in an area where other ships might anchor or fishermen might trawl, is a wreck symbol on a chart.

But it is a different story if the ship was carrying a consignment of gold or silver, tin, copper or lead, all of which, in greater or lesser degree, are well worth the expenditure of time, money and effort in attempted recovery. In 1969, gold was worth about £551,000 a ton; at the other end of the scale, the value of a ton of lead was a mere £130 but still worthwhile if the salvage operations promise to be fairly simple and straight-forward.

If a ship is merely stranded on a mud or sand bank or on a beach, and is undamaged, refloating usually presents no great problem, especially if in tidal waters and if the stranding occurred at a state of the tide when it is only necessary to wait for the next high water to refloat her of its own accord.

In the open ocean the tidal range, which is the difference between the level of the sea at low and high water, is only about four feet but, of course, ships do not often become stranded in the open ocean. Stranding usually occurs in channels or coastal waters where the height of the tidal range is much greater than in the open sea. The greatest tidal range in the world is in the Bay of Fundy in Nova Scotia, where the dif-ference between high and low water may be as much as 70 feet, but this extreme augmentation of the tidal wave at spring tides is simply due to a large body of moving water being confined in a narrowing funnel.

Spring tides, of course, have nothing to do with Spring the season. It is a name adapted from a Norse word meaning 'swelling' and is given to the tides which occur just after full and change of moon, when tides rise higher and fall lower than when the sun and moon are at right angles in relation to the earth. The tidal range is then much less because the attraction of the moon is opposed to that of the sun, and the tides at this time are termed *neaps*, from another Norse word meaning 'scarcity'.

In the Bristol Channel at Avonmouth, spring tides have an extreme range of 45 feet, and in the English Channel the difference between high and low water at springs varies between 38 feet at the western end, in the Channel Islands, and 24 feet at Dover. The tidal range at neap tides is, generally, a little over one third of the range at springs.

But even the 70 foot tides of the Bay of Fundy are dwarfed into insignificance by the greatest sea wave of all time. In August 1883, a terrific submarine eruption beneath the centre of the island of Krakatoa in the Strait of Sunda produced a gigantic sea wave which travelled half-way round the world. It

18

reached the almost unbelievable height of 135 feet and most of the tide gauges in the world recorded the disturbance. Its effects were actually observed on the tide gauge at Havre, 11,000 miles from Krakatoa.

Quite ordinary rough sea waves sometimes reach an enormous height after striking against a sea wall or other vertical structure, and exert a terrific force. In the winter of 1861, during a violent storm, the fog bell on Bishop Rock lighthouse, off the Isles of Scilly, was broken off by a huge wave which roared up the lighthouse as high as the gallery, 100 feet above sea level. The bell was connected to the gallery by an iron bar four inches thick which snapped like a matchstick. After the storm the gallery was found strewn with sand.

If a ship goes aground at, or near, high tide or in almost tideless waters, then the only way of refloating her is by lightening the vessel in some way. If she is already 'light', that is, unloaded, this may sometimes be effected by pumping out ballast water or fuel oil, or by discharging bunker coal; if loaded, by shifting or discharging cargo. In some instances, the actual level of the water may be raised by a change of wind and a stranded vessel refloated with very little assistance, even when the tidal range is too small to be of any material help.

In 1922, a small cargo ship, the *King David*, was refloated in this manner. After loading about 5,500 tons of grain at Santa Fé on the River Parana, some 320 miles above Buenos Aires in South America, she moved down river to Rosario, where the water is deeper, to take on the remaining 3,000 tons of cargo. Fully loaded and drawing about 21 feet of water, she left Rosario, homeward bound, on December 15th, and continued down river in fine calm weather. There had been little or no wind for several weeks and the water level, which depends largely on the force and direction of the wind, was lower than normal. In the River Plate, a north or north-westerly wind of about 15 knots may lower the water level by one and a half feet; if such a wind suddenly changes to the opposite direction, the level can rise by as much as three feet in an hour.

The River Parana flows into the River Uruguay about 74 miles from Buenos Aires and, just after midnight, as *King David* approached Martin Garcia, about 17 miles below the junction of the Parana and Uruguay rivers, the pilot said to the 'old man'—to merchant seamen the master is always the 'old man' whatever his age, never the 'captain'—"There's a ship aground on the Martin Garcia bar. What do you want to do— anchor?" The old man, no doubt fearing the wrath of the ship's owners if he delayed unnecessarily by anchoring, replied "If she's not drawing more than us, we'll chance it", meaning 'if we don't need more water to float in than she does, we'll get over all right if we keep in the deepest part of the channel'. She crept towards the grounded vessel, barely maintaining steerage way, until she got within hailing distance. It was a still dark night, without a breath of wind, and sounds carried far over the glassy smooth water. "What is your draft?" the pilot shouted through the megaphone—there were no electronic amplifiers in those days. "Twenty-two feet" came the answer. "Right," said the old man, "cross the bar at the deepest part and we'll make it." "Slow ahead, then" said the pilot, and she gathered way again, heading towards the middle of the channel. The white anchor lights and two all-round red lights, one above the other, of the other vessel, signifying a vessel aground, showed clear and bright as the *King David* approached her. She steamed on. Now the other vessel was abeam, barely 200 yards away, and the old man heaved a sigh of relief as she passed astern. Then "Half speed ahead" ordered the pilot, and "Wheel to port" to bring her round in the right direction, but there was no answering movement of the ship's head. "Full ahead", and she started coming round, and then stopped. She had touched bottom—smoothly and gently, without any bump.

By going full ahead, and alternately hard a-port and hard a-starboard with the wheel, she managed to slither across the sand bank into deeper water, but by then she was close to the bank on the other side of the channel, so the pilot ordered "Half speed astern" to back into the channel again—and that was her undoing. She touched bottom for the second time that night, but this time her stern was well and truly stuck. No amount of "Full ahead, hard a-port", "Stop", "Hard a-starboard, full ahead" would budge her. They sounded round the ship and found that the bow was still afloat in 24 feet of water, but astern there was only 20 feet on one side and 19 feet on the other. Up went their anchor lights, and two red lights amidships. They were there for the rest of the night, anyway.

By morning there was a freshening wind from the north; the temperature was rising, but pressure was falling slowly and they knew that a *pampero* was on its way. This is the name given to the strong squally wind from the south or south-west which follows the passage of a cold front in the River Plate. Before the arrival of the cold front the weather becomes very oppressive and the air is sometimes filled with myriads of insects. Following the frontal passage, the temperature falls and pressure rises, and a strong squally wind blows for two or three days, with gusts reaching a speed of 70 knots or more, instantaneously, and accompanied by torrential rain.

By the following afternoon the water level had fallen by another foot. Twenty-four hours later, the tips of two propeller blades were showing above water and the ship was hard and fast aground from stem to stern.

A tug summoned from Buenos Aires next morning carried out her starboard anchor and dropped it in deep water. Then the old man went back in the tug to Buenos Aires to make arrangements for 2,000 tons of cargo to be discharged into lighters. It was December 19th and they were looking forward with some pleasure to spending Christmas in port, reloading—instead of 'harking to the herald angels' in the middle of the ocean on Christmas Day.

Late that afternoon there was a sudden lull in the weather; the wind switched to the south-west and started to blow again. By midnight it was up to 30 knots; the sea was white with breaking crests and the water level was rising fast. By 1.30 a.m. her bow was afloat and the ship became like a wild animal, with its hind legs caught in a trap and its fore feet clawing at the ground, trying to pull itself free. As each oncoming sea lifted her bow, and clouds of spray swept along her starboard side and across the deck like heavy driving rain, she would heave one way and then the other as the trough passed, pivoting on her stern which was still aground. A great shudder ran right through the ship as she touched bottom again.

Between squalls, they managed to heave in a few feet of anchor cable, pulling her bow into deeper and deeper water.

Just before daybreak she floated free and she weighed anchor; steamed down to Buenos Aires, picked up the old man and set off, once more, for home—6,500 miles away. They had Christmas at sea after all, but goose for dinner; they must have been very cheap in Rosario, otherwise it would have been the same old corned beef which was their normal Sunday 'joint' in those days. On weekdays, it was alternately salt beef and dried peas one day, and salt pork with haricot beans the next. Their fresh water tanks were filled up from the river, with a 50-cigarette tin of permanganate of potash in each tank to kill the River Plate bugs. It's a wonder the author is alive to tell the tale.

Not all stranded ships are pulled off as easily as that, and without damage. If a vessel has run aground at high water on a sand bank or gently sloping beach, and the tidal range is such that, at low water, she is high and dry, refloating her is not necessarily a very difficult operation. Even if she has been holed, any water inside will run out as the tide falls. Minor leaks can be stopped with wooden plugs or wedges, and steel or wooden patches can be fitted over the larger holes.

To prevent a stranded ship from going farther aground, or being turned sideways by on-shore winds at subsequent high tides, anchors can be carried out seaward into deeper water and the cables kept taut to prevent her being moved. Heavy anchors can then be laid out in deep water with wire ropes leading to the ship's own winches. A high mechanical advantage can be obtained with this 'beach gear', as it is called, by using a 3-fold purchase—two pulley blocks, each with three sheaves—so that a 10-ton pull on the hauling part will produce a 60-ton pull on the anchor. If less power is available and the hauling part is rove in a 4-fold purchase, with another 4-fold purchase on the hauling part, a pull of only one ton on the ship's winch will produce a 60-ton pull on the anchor. In suitable cases the depth of water can be increased by dredging a channel in the direction in which the ship will be hauled off, and tugs, trimmed by the stern can be used alongside to scour away the bottom by working their propellers.

During heaving-off operations it sometimes helps if the salvage vessel or tug, with a tow wire attached, sweeps laterally

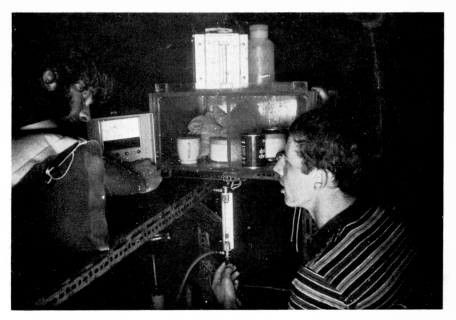

Plate 3a and b,
The underwater
'house'

Plate 4a,
Four-inch air lift

b, c and d,
Views of Ship's Side cut from wreck

to help break the suction on the sea bed, or a secondary set of beach gear is rigged at right angles to the primary set and alternately hauled in and slacked off to increase the wrenching movement.

If a ship has been sunk in water deep enough for her to be completely submerged at all times, then salvage operations are, at the best, difficult and, at the worst, impossible. In fact, except where the wreck is a navigational hazard—or in rare instances, such as in the case of the scuttled German fleet at Scapa Flow, when the scrap value made even difficult, expensive and protracted salvage operations profitable—it is only the recovery of valuable cargo which is normally attempted.

A sunken ship is, of course, always full, or almost full, of water, invariably holed, sometimes considerably battered, and may be in any position between upright and completely upside down, depending on whether she foundered through collision, fire, explosion, mine, torpedo or by capsizing due to deck damage or cargo shifting in rough weather.

In cases where salvage is to be attempted, a complete survey of the wreck by experienced divers must first be made so that the precise angle at which the vessel is lying, the extent of the damage and the size of the holes may be established. It can then be decided whether the ship can be raised by pumping out the water or by the use of compressed air, or a combination of both. If she is resting upright on the sea bed, but has extensive bottom damage, she cannot be refloated by pumping because the bottom is inaccessible for patching. But if the main deck is less than 35 feet down, it may be possible to raise her by using compressed air, if the ship's side and main deck are strong enough to withstand the increased pressure.

Before a sunken vessel can be raised by pumping out the water, the hull must, of course, be made watertight. Small leaks which are within the reach of a diver can be stopped with wooden plugs or special leak-stopping compounds.

For cracks and small holes which are inaccessible, some rather primitive but nevertheless effective methods are often adopted, such as feeding in sawdust, straw or oakum while water is pumped out from an adjacent compartment. The flow of water through the hole will carry the material towards it where it will lodge, swell up, and eventually stop the leak, in the same way that a small heap of rust particles will gather over a pin-hole in the bottom of a domestic water tank and completely seal the perforation, or a face-cloth left in an emptying bath will be drawn into the plug hole and stop the water running out.

Small patches are usually constructed of two layers of planking nailed together at right angles, or of 2-inch tongued and grooved boards on a 4 by 4-inch frame, while patches for larger holes are made of wood, iron or reinforced cement, or a combination of all three. Concrete, too, made with very little water so that the mixture is fairly dry, is frequently used. The hole may first be stuffed with such ready made plugs such as pillows, blankets or mattresses, and cement or concrete poured in through a pipe with a funnel end protruding just above water. The whole mass sets hard and effectively seals the aperture.

Very large patches are made of heavy tongued and grooved planking which, in extreme cases, may be as much as 20 inches thick. The timbers are spiked to a heavy frame, but such out-size patches are usually made to the shape of a previously constructed template, built ashore, and then taken out and lowered into position. After being drawn into place by tackles rigged inside the sunken ship, the frame is bolted to the hull plating—no easy task for divers working under water. Afterwards, as the water level inside the ship is lowered by pumping, the great pressure outside forces the patch tight against the hull and makes it watertight.

A cofferdam is a watertight barrier erected to exclude water when the foundations of a bridge or pier are being constructed. In salvage operations on a wreck in shallow water, cofferdams—extending to just above the surface at high water—are erected round openings in the deck, or a huge single barrier may be built round the whole perimeter of the deck. Then, when all patching has been completed and pumping operations commence, the water is first pumped out of the cofferdam, and then out of the ship itself, until positive buoyancy is obtained and the vessel rises.

A wreck which is upside down does not necessarily present a more difficult salvage proposition; the deciding factor may well be the extent and position of the hull damage. If, for instance, she is upside down in shallow water and only her hatches have been stove in, or damage is confined to the deck area, all that needs to be done, broadly speaking, is to blow out enough water to restore positive buoyancy and she will come to the surface—like some gigantic diving bell. The openings in the deck will have provided natural outlets for the escape of water as the vessel rises, to balance the decreasing pressure outside.

But, of course, it is never quite so simple as that. The distribution of the induced buoyancy has to be carefully calculated and controlled, and de-watering of the various compartments carried out in a strictly pre-planned order so that the upturned vessel does not list heavily on the way up.

The appearance on the surface of bubbles approximately outlining the shape of the wreck is an indication that the bottom suction is about to be broken and, once this is complete and the vessel acquires positive buoyancy, she will rise very rapidly. This period is the most critical phase of the whole operation, and if she takes on a list which becomes uncontrolled she could spill out the air, turn over and sink again, with almost certain disaster for the salvage vessel above.

The use of air is not, however, the most common method adopted to raise a vessel, because of the many inherent difficulties connected with this type of salvage operation which do not arise when other methods are being used. For instance, a much higher standard of repair is required, as nearly five times more air than water will escape from around a patch which is not absolutely tight, or through a hole or crack which has remained undetected. There is also greater risk of the hull fracturing as the vessel rises, due to the increasing difference between internal and external pressures.

Steel tubes containing air-tight sections fitted with access hatches, known as 'air-locks', have also to be erected and secured to the hull of the wreck so that men can get down into the vessel to effect repairs. Each air-lock must be high enough for the top to be above water at all times, and structures as much as 130 feet high, 4 feet across at the top, 7 feet at the base, and weighing up to 30 tons have actually been used. One can well imagine the dangers and problems divers have to face when installing such enormous air-locks as these.

If the wrecked ship has a damaged bottom, but is otherwise intact and still upright, or if she is completely upside down, but with only minor bottom damage, then de-watering by compressed air is often the easiest method to adopt. In the former case, the holes in the bottom become ready-made vents for the escape of water as air is pumped in, and later when the pressure of the water outside becomes less as the vessel rises. In the second instance, there is, probably a certain amount of air still trapped inside the hull, and some compartments may even be intact with no water at all in them.

In any case, when raising a vessel by compressed air, bottom vents are essential. If there are none, or the few which do exist are confined to one area, holes must be cut so that each compartment, or group of compartments, may be de-watered as required and the trim of the wreck strictly controlled.

Lifting a vessel by mechanical means is generally carried out in conjunction with one or more of the other methods of salvaging, and is mainly used because of its greater control over the vessel's stability while being raised. The operation of getting the lifting wires in position under the wreck may be a simple matter of first using a small boat to drag a light wire underneath the hull. A larger wire is then attached to the end of this small wire—or 'messenger', as it is called—and drawn through. Finally, the lifting wire itself, which may be as large as nine inches in circumference with a breaking strain of 250 tons, is heaved through and both ends connected to hauling wires over the bow of the lifting vessel. The operation is repeated until several slings are in position and the weight adequately distributed.

But it is seldom as simple as it sounds. If the wreck is upside down, partly buried or on a rough bottom, getting the lifting wires underneath may prove an extremely difficult operation requiring the employment of divers. If the bottom is soft mud or sand, a tunnel for the messenger may be washed out beneath the wreck by the salvage vessel, using a hose and a mixture of air and water.

Two lifting vessels sometimes work together, one on each

side, with the slings in pairs; one leading from the port side of one vessel, down under the wreck, and up to the starboard side of the other vessel, and vice versa.

In tidal waters, the lift provided by the tide is used to its fullest advantage. At low water the lifting wires are tightened and secured and bottom suction is broken as the tide commences to rise. At high water, the sunken vessel can be moved towards the shore and the operation repeated on each subsequent tide until she is in a position where repairs can be carried out and the vessel refloated

A device known as an 'air-lift' is sometimes used to remove sand or mud from around a stranded vessel, or from a sunken wreck. Air bubbles rising in water exert a tremendous lifting force and will bring with them to the surface quite large particles of other matter. As, for instance, when cooking peas and bubbles of air produced by the boiling water rise from the bottom of the saucepan and up to the surface; if the saucepan is nearly full, the mixture will boil over, the rising bubbles of air carrying the peas right up to the top and over the side. If a short length of pipe is placed upright in the saucepan so that the bottom end is among the peas and the top is above the water, and air is introduced into the lower end of the pipe by means of a pump, instead of boiling the water, the same thing will happen because the mixture of air and water will be less dense than the water outside the pipe and will, therefore, rise to the top, carrying the peas with it.

The analogy is, no doubt, obvious. Enlarge the pipe to about 12 inches in diameter, make it long enough for the bottom end to be submerged in the sand or mud, with the air pipe connected to it about a foot or so from the bottom, and the sand or mud—or even pebbles and larger pieces of material —will begin rising as soon as the air is turned on. (Plate 4a.)

Air-lifts are also used in cargo recovery, especially in cases where a valuable mineral cargo is in small pieces, as with some ores, and becomes scattered in the wreck or on the sea bed.

CHAPTER THREE

SEARCHING TECHNIQUES

'To catch a monkey you first have to find it' is an adage of undisputed truth. Similarly, if it is a wreck you want to 'catch', that too must first be found—though, unlike the monkey, it cannot run away and hide somewhere else. Where it sinks it stays, but even so searching for a wreck is likely to be even more difficult and frustrating than looking for the proverbial monkey.

When a ship goes down its position is, of course, of vital importance to those on board, as otherwise their chances of being rescued are greatly diminished. If the disaster occurs within sight of land, its precise position may well be known, but more often than not there is considerable doubt as to the exact location of a wreck. In fact, only where part of the vessel remains above water is the position absolutely certain. There was, for example, no doubt at all about the positions of most of the ships of the German fleet scuttled in Scapa Flow on June 21st, 1919, for here the water was not deep enough even to cover the hulls of some of the larger vessels.

In deeper water, but near enough to land for accurate bearings to be taken when time permits, the position can be pin-pointed with some certainty, but even so an error of one degree in a bearing will produce a position error of over 500 feet only 5 miles from the land, and proportionately more for greater distances. In fact, the only method of accurately plotting the position, other than by taking horizontal sextant angles with a sextant between three suitably selected charted objects— rarely practicable when a ship is sinking—is by 'transits', where conspicuous points ashore which are also marked on the chart or can be pictorially recorded and preserved, and are suitably positioned, are observed to be in line. If two such transits about 90 degrees apart are observed, an extremely accurate position is established at their point of intersection.

Only a minority of wrecks occur in such convenient places. In most instances the reported position of a sinking, calculated from the last known fix which may have been hours, or even days, previously can be—and usually is—up to 10 or even 20 or more miles in error. That means a search area of 100 or even 400 or more square miles, respectively, and the fact that the object of the search may be under hundreds of feet of water does not make the task any easier.

Searching for a wreck in 400 square miles is like looking for a pocket wallet on a flooded football field, and if the football field is under 20 feet of water and there are dozens of other objects of similar size and shape scattered about, looking for a particular one is, obviously, no easy matter.

Some searches last for years. Once the limits of the search area have been established, the position of every wreck found in that area must be plotted as accurately as possible and then, starting with the one which most nearly resembles in size the particular vessel being searched for, each one must be examined by divers and details compared with those of the vessel concerned.

The old fashioned method was to sweep the sea bed with a weighted wire rope slung between two vessels—a slow and tedious operation resulting in many false 'catches'. Even if the precise position of the wreck is known, a mere 50 foot lane of unswept sea bed could result in quite a moderate-sized ship being missed entirely. If it is absolutely certain that the area being swept contains the wreck, that area must be gone over thoroughly, and then searched again if necessary until the wreck is found. It is no good giving up and trying somewhere else. Many years ago, in the days of the old compressed-air driven torpedoes, a torpedo on trials had failed to surface. It just went on down and stuck fast in the mud but continued to send up a stream of air bubbles long enough for it to be plotted by a shore station and the position marked with a buoy.

Next day two launches began sweeping. A small area was centred on the marker buoy was laid out, the marker buoy was taken up and the boats went in. Days went by with no luck. Several times the sweep was caught up but slipped free without bringing anything to the surface; and Headquarters, knowing nothing about the practical difficulties of sweeping for a comparatively small object in tidal waters, became exasperated at the delay and sent down a chairborne Lieutenant to investigate. He went out on one of the sweeping launches, bent on 'sorting things out' and getting results. He probably had ideas of catching the afternoon train back and being able to get to his office in time to send the Commander home with news that 'he had found the thing within an hour'.

After nearly three hours of unsuccessful sweeping in the marked area, he said to the coxswain "Look, Sergeant, it obviously is not here. What about trying over there?" The chairborne Lieutenant had already annoyed the crew by his own quite obvious dissatisfaction with their efforts so far, and his thoughts may, perhaps, be imagined when his vision of catching the afternoon train back, with his halo in his brief case, was shattered by the coxswain replying "Look, Sir, if you'll excuse me saying so, Sir, if we can't find it where we know it bloody well is, we won't find it where we know it bloody well ain't, now will we, Sir?"

That was only a torpedo, but when sweeping for a ship the same basic principles apply. Everything the sweep gets really caught up on must be surveyed by divers and because many of the 'snags' inevitably turn out to be hitherto uncharted rock patches or other unwanted obstructions, it is, generally speaking, a rather uneconomical method of searching for a wreck; though both the *Egypt*, which went down after a collision off Ushant in 1922 and the *Niagara*, sunk by an enemy mine off New Zealand in 1940 were eventually located by sweeping.

Probably the two most useful aids to wreck location are Asdic and the Echo Sounder. Sound waves in water travel at about 5,000 feet per second, or approximately five times faster than in air, and both Asdic and Echo Sounder make use of this property to locate objects and inequalities on the sea bed, to measure and record their height and extent and, in the case of Asdic, their distances and direction from the operating vessel.

One can measure, roughly, the distance of a hillside by shouting at it from across a valley and then counting the seconds between the shout and the return of the echo. Broadly speaking, both Asdic and Echo Sounders measure distances in the same way except, of course, they do not just 'shout'.

Asdic was originally designed as an anti-submarine device. The name itself is, in fact, formed from the initial letters of the body set up by the Allies after the 1914-18 war to devise methods of detecting submarines—the Allied Submarine Detection Investigation Committee. Later, when only Britain and America remained interested in the investigation, the 'Allied' was changed to 'Anti' but this did not affect the name Asdic. Briefly, it is a device which, by means of an electrically motivated oscillator, sends a beam of sound waves through the water. When these strike an object on the sea bed they are reflected back again, just as the shout was reflected back from the hillside or the beam of light from an electric torch locates an object by reflected light waves.

The Asdic beam is electrically controlled to operate through 360 degrees horizontally, and the returning sound is amplified so that both distance and direction of the reflecting object can be accurately recorded—accurately, that is, with certain reservations.

The speed of sound in water varies with different densities and temperatures, the waves travelling faster in warmer layers and slower in colder layers or where density is greater through increased salinity or the concentration of plankton. These influences cause the beam to bend. In extreme cases, a layer of warm water with colder water both above and below can cause the Asdic beam to run horizontally along the warm layer and then back to the surface, so that very few sound waves penetrate to the sea bed. Or if the water gets progressively colder downwards, the beam is bent so much by being slowed down by the colder water that, in addition to producing poor quality echoes, the recorded direction and distance of a wreck or other object may be much in error. With these reservations, Asdic can be a valuable wreck locator.

The main, central, narrow beam of pulses has a range of about 2 miles under good conditions and a surrounding beam of lower frequency which has a wider angle and goes deeper has an effective range of between 1,500 and 2,000 yards, about half that of the main beam. The Asdic machine, which far from being a shining, streamlined example of modern electronic equipment, has all the appearance of a rather ancient home-made typewriter with a few strings attached, produces a paper record of the pattern and range of the echoes. Analysis of the 'trace' by an experienced Asdic operator will give valuable additional information regarding the general state of the wreck or whatever is sending back the echoes. A broken down and scattered wreck, for instance, will return long indefinite echoes, whereas sharp and well-defined echoes would indicate a more solid and less ragged object—which could well turn out to be a rock peak instead of something more interesting. But the pattern of rock echoes is usually, though not always, sufficiently different to be clearly distinguishable from wreck echoes.

They were not, for instance, on more than one occasion during the great search in the Irish Sea for the missing proto-type Victor Mark II bomber in 1960. After spending hours mooring up right over a 'very promising contact' which had been found by Asdic, the salvage vessel started grabbing to try and recover part of the object for identification purposes, only to find, after several more hours work, that she was biting the middle out of a ridge of clay and rock. Asdic conditions were, however, unusually bad at the time, and in any case everything even remotely promising had to be investigated. Nobody knew, at that time, what the remains of the Victor—if remains there were—were going to look like.

When searching for an ordinary wreck, however, once the existence of a suspicious object on the sea bed has been estab-lished by Asdic, and provided its position, extent and pattern justifies further examination, it is usually at this stage that the Echo Sounder is brought into use. This is another recording device which also transmits a beam of sound waves into the water; but unlike Asdic it sends out a near-horizontal beam, which goes downwards so that the electrically transmitted sound waves strike the sea bed directly beneath the vessel. The time taken for the pulses to reach the bottom and return to the ship is automatically transformed into a distance, or depth in this case, and recorded on a moving strip of paper.

Echo sounders usually operate on two different phases of range and speed; a high-speed range using a scale of 0–630 feet takes 200 soundings per minute and records the depth in feet, while the low-speed range covering depths up to 630 fathoms with 33 soundings per minute, records the depth in fathoms. With either the feet or fathoms scale in use, the paper record shows a continuous contour of the sea bed directly beneath the vessel as it moves along and provides for 120 hours of continuous recording. (Plate 5a.)

The pulsed wave transmissions used in Echo Sounders also rebound from shoals of fish, and another type of sounder specially designed for fishing vessels has a range of 1,300 fathoms, which is 7,800 feet and more than one and a quarter nautical miles.

A more advanced type of under-water sound equipment known as a Transit Sonar, produced by Kelvin Hughes, has been specially designed for hydrographic survey and the location of wrecks and other obstructions. Instead of the transmitted sound waves going straight down to the bottom directly below the operating vessel, the fan-shaped-beam, very narrow horizontally—is thrown on to the sea bed to one side of the vessel's track. It operates on two range scales, 0–900 feet at 160 transmissions per minute and 0–1,800 feet at 80 transmissions. The beam strikes the sea bed in the same way as a light shining through a slit in a curtain shows a long narrow patch of light on the ground outside.

As the vessel moves along, echoes received back from the sea bed are built up into a visual picture of the contours of the bottom as the beam passes over it, and of any obstruction superimposed on the bottom, such as a wreck or other obstruction. The absence of echoes from the far side of any wreck shows on the record as a white shadow and from this, under good conditions, the approximate height, size and direction in which the wreck is lying can be estimated. (Plate 5b.)

33

Having located a hopeful wreck by Asdic, and guided by the Asdic beam, the searching vessel steams slowly over the position from different directions. As she passes over the wreck the apparent depth of water being recorded by the Echo Sounder is immediately reduced by the height of the wreck and the trace shows a sharp peak. If this height, or 'lift', of the wreck above the sea bed compares favourably with the dimensions of the vessel being searched for, further examination, in the form of a diver's survey, is usually necessary before its identity can be definitely established.

But a ship cannot just stop in the open sea and send a diver down to look at a wreck. Apart from the vagaries of the weather there are usually tides or currents to contend with, and even in calm and tideless waters a ship must be held stationary in some way to prevent her drifting out of position before the diving operations can start, and to prevent her moving after the diver has gone down, so that he is in no danger of finding himself suddenly becoming entangled in what may turn out to be just a twisted mass of jagged, torn and rusty steel.

Not only must the salvage ship be moored so that she can remain in one position for as long as necessary, but she must also be able to put the diver down in any one particular spot and, once he is down, to move him in any required direction a few feet at a time. Just anchoring the ship would not be the slightest use, and so, before any diver's survey can be carried out, the salvage ship must lay her moorings.

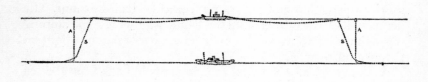

An elevational diagram of the salvage vessel moored above the wreck lying on the sea bed 400 feet below. Head and stern moorings only are shown. The buoys when laid would be in position 'A'. When the vessel is moored, the buoys would be in position 'B'.

After pin-pointing the exact position of the wreck by dropping a marker buoy on the spot, either four or six heavy moorings are usually laid round the marker buoy at about 450 to 500 yards radius. For an average-sized sea-going salvage vessel working in depths of 40 to 60 fathoms, that is 240 to 300 feet,

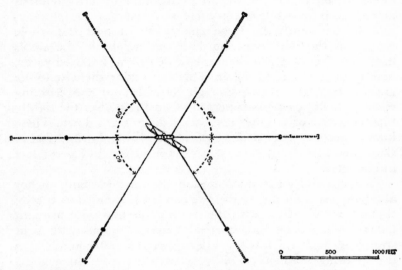

A typical 6-point mooring showing lay-out of the moorings and the salvage vessel moored in position over a wreck. The vessel is lying head to prevailing wind or strongest tide, with the heavier mooring ahead, and to the left of the diagram.

or more each mooring would consist of a heavy anchor of between four and six tons in weight, between 270 and 450 feet of chain cable, with a length of three-inch circumference wire rope from the chain cable to the mooring buoy itself. The wire pendant would be about 30 feet less than the depth of water in which the mooring was to be laid, so that all the wear caused by rise and fall of tide or other movements of the buoy—which subject a part of the mooring to continuous wear on the sea bed—is borne by the chain and not by the wire.

The moored vessel would always endeavour to lie head on to the prevailing wind and sea and, in the case of a six-point moor, the head mooring would be the one with the heavier, six-ton anchor. There would be another mooring on each bow, 60 degrees either side of the head mooring and one on each quarter, 60 degrees either side of the stern mooring, so that the moored vessel, with a wire rope to each of the six buoys, can move herself in any desired direction and by any required amount as little as two or three feet if necessary.

The buoys must be large enough to support the whole weight of the wire pendant, half the weight of the ship's mooring wire, of which there might be several hundred yards, and up to 30 feet of the chain cable connecting the wire to the anchor, and also strong enough to withstand the crushing effect of being deeply submerged when the pull of the tightly moored vessel or weather conditions drags them down. These buoys, therefore, are usually conically ended and cylindrical in shape and may be as much as 10 feet in height and 4 or 5 feet in diameter.

Each mooring is first made up complete on deck. Both anchor and buoy are hoisted over the side and left suspended on special slipping attachments, with the chain cable and wire pendant flaked out on deck and secured at various points with light strands of rope which will break in turn, one after another, as the mooring runs out. This prevents the whole thing going over the side already tied up in knots.

When the first mooring is ready, the vessel steams slowly in towards the marker buoy carefully checking its range and bearing, for each mooring will be laid to conform with a pre-arranged pattern. At the precise moment when range and bearing indicate that the vessel is in position, the anchor is slipped and drops down to the bottom, dragging the chain cable and wire after it. As the ship is still moving slowly through the water when the anchor hits the sea bed, both anchor and chain cable are laid out in the right direction, thus ensuring that the complete mooring is properly laid for the subsequent pull of the moored ship.

Just before the wire pendant runs out, the buoy is slipped and the vessel then sheers away clear and lays off while the next mooring is made up ready for dropping.

Six moorings must be laid if the survey is intended to be

anything more than a brief superficial examination; for only when the vessel is able to move in any direction and under absolute control can the diver in his observation chamber, suspended above or alongside the wreck and on the end of two or three hundred feet of wire rope, make an adequate survey. When all six moorings are in position, wire ropes are run out from the salvage vessel and secured to the buoys in turn and then, in the centre of this thousand-yard diameter six-spoked wheel, like a spider in the middle of its web, the ship takes up her position directly over the wreck. The marker buoy, now close alongside, is taken aboard and—down goes the observation chamber.

The diver's initial survey may require nothing more complicated than just 'having a look'. Under ideal conditions and once the wreck has been marked, the whole operation including laying the moorings could be completed in a day, for a few minutes observation by the diver may be sufficient for the searching vessel to discard that particular wreck for good. Then, all that remains to be done is to lift the moorings—and move on to the next one.

Some years ago, the search for a First World War wreck, south-west of the Isles of Scilly, with several thousand tons of copper on board and therefore worth looking for—an operation which had already lasted through the summer seasons of several years during which time more than seventy wrecks had been found and surveyed—was extended southwards. The survivors of the lost vessel had taken to the boats when the ship was sunk, and sailed towards the Islands, directed by the German submarine commander. The official position of the sinking had differed from that obtained from the German submarine records by about 15 miles, and the original search area had been calculated to include both of these positions and that deduced from the survivors' estimates of how far, how long and in what general direction they had sailed or rowed before being picked up by a passing ship nearer the Scillies. A second lifeboat, which had become separated from the other during the first night after the sinking, had actually reached the Islands several days later.

Asdic and Echo Sounder had picked up a wreck which was

near enough the right size and height to justify a diver's survey, so moorings were laid, the salvage ship positioned right over the wreck and the diver went down in an observation chamber to have a look. The depth was about 380 feet. Under-water visibility was, fortunately, excellent and when about 20 feet from the sea bed and close to one side of the wreck, the diver's voice came up over the telephone to the bridge of the salvage vessel more than 350 feet above him: "Hold the chamber." Then five minutes silence while he accustomed his eyes to under-water looking and then, instead of getting an order to 'Lower chamber 5 feet' or 'Move 6 feet to port' or some other similar request, the silence was broken by his voice saying "Up chamber—the sea bed is littered with Sherman tanks." Proof enough that the latest find was of the wrong period for no First World War wreck could have possibly had any Sherman tanks on board to take to the bottom with her.

Not all surveys are as quick or as easy as that. Most require hours of looking, moving a few feet at a time right round the wreck, observing positions of masts, sizes of hatches, numbers of derricks and any other details which may be compared with the general arrangement drawings of the original ship which, if they still existed, would be on board the salvage vessel.

If the wreck is fairly whole and in an upright position on the sea bed, it may sometimes be identified almost at once—even without the Sherman tanks or any other datable cargo. As, for instance, if the vessel being searched for is a flush-decked ship and the wreck under survey has a raised forecastle, bridge section and poop. But, of course, not every wreck is still in one piece or remains conveniently upright on the sea bed as if it had just gone down there for a rest. The disaster which has sent her to the bottom has usually resulted in quite a lot of hull damage, and even if this is confined to a large hole in the bottom or side, such as might be caused by the ship striking a rock, or being involved in a collision, hitting a mine or being torpedoed, she is invariably damaged in one way or another by the time she reaches her last resting place on the sea bed.

In some cases, what the diver sees when he first goes down bears little resemblance to a once proud ship. The fore part of the wreck may be almost upside down with the mast, ventilators and bridge twisted and broken, or crushed flat, with every once recognizable feature obliterated in a tortuous mass of rusty ironwork. Then, perhaps, a great gaping hole with most of the ship's side and bottom torn open as if by a giant tin opener—and the rest of her, what was once the stern, lying on its side but now a mere shapeless mass.

The only course then may be to cut out a huge square from her side or bottom, large enough to include several plates and frames. This sample is then hoisted up from the wreck, now more mutilated than before, and laid out on the deck of the salvage vessel where the size and thickness of her plates, rivet spacings and the depth and thickness of her frames can be measured and compared with the drawings. (Plate 4 *b*, *c* and *d*.)

This blasting out of a section of shell plating from a badly damaged wreck entails days, or even weeks, of tedious but highly skilled work for the divers. The gelignite charges must be carefully and accurately placed in position under directions from the diver in his observation chamber, and when both 'bomb' and diver are swinging about on the end of several hundred feet of wire, ten feet or so apart—like twin pendulums, the one trying to direct someone else operating a winch on the deck of the vessel hundreds of feet above him to lower the charge on to one particular spot on the sloping side of a wreck—the accurate and successful placing of each charge becomes a feat in itself.

Days of work may be involved, interrupted perhaps by bad weather which compels the salvage vessel to slip moorings and run for shelter to the nearest port or ride out a gale at sea, and then wait for the swell to die down before mooring up again and resuming the operation. Only to find, in the end, when the piece is at last cut free and hoisted on deck, that it does not 'fit' after all—and one more heap of remains is relegated to the list of wrong wrecks.

When a large number of unidentified wrecks is found in the search area, it is a waste of time going to the trouble of laying moorings, and surveying them willy-nilly, and spending several days looking at each one as soon as it is located. Economically, the most likely one must be surveyed first and it is therefore necessary to plot each wreck, mark its position in some way and then, when the search area has been thoroughly covered, to decide on some order of priority for surveying.

In a search area 20 miles square, which is not far short of three times the size of the Isle of Wight, it is quite impracticable to lay a marker buoy on every wreck which justifies further investigation. Any buoys left until the good weather season the following year would be either out of position or missing altogether by the time operations could be resumed. The area may also straddle a shipping lane, with dire results for passing ships as well as for the marker buoys themselves especially on dark nights. How, then, can the position of something on the sea bed be so accurately recorded that a ship can go back to it any time and be sure of finding it without having to go again through all the ramifications of the original search?

Position fixing by nautical astronomy, besides being quite impracticable also in most cases for the simple reason that a salvage ship cannot afford just to remain over a wreck waiting for clear skies and suitable conditions for an astronomical fix, is not accurate enough for the purpose. It is no good being several hundred yards out, and even a few hundred feet in error would require the resumption of some measure of searching.

The accuracy of astronomical observations depends primarily on the accurate measuring of the altitude of the sun or a star or planet at a particular instant. An error of only one second of angle, which is one 3,600th part of a degree, can produce an error in distance of 100 feet, while a mistake of one second in time could result in a distance error of as much as a quarter of a mile. In certain areas, however, means of pinpointing a wreck, and without resorting to any visual marker, do exist.

Around the coasts of north-west Europe from Norway to south-west Portugal, off the eastern seaboard of Canada and the United States of America from Newfoundland to Virginia, and in the Persian Gulf the Decca Navigator System enables any vessel which is equipped with the necessary radio receiver and which is also operating within the areas covered by the system, to establish its position at any time of the day or night, irrespective of visibility and quite independently of astronomical observations, with considerable accuracy.

Special radio transmitting stations at a number of selected

points on land are arranged in groups of four, with a 'Master'
station in the centre and three 'Slave' stations equidistant from
the centre and forming a sort of three-spoked wheel. The distance from hub to rim may be anything between 60 and 120
miles, depending on local radio propagation conditions and
coverage requirements.

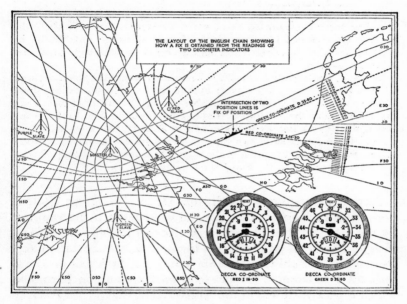

Decca transmissions are unmodulated continuous-wave low frequency
signals from groups of land-based stations. There are four to a standard
group of Chain, a centrally placed master with Red, Green and Purple
Slaves sited 80 to 100 miles from it in star formation. Transmissions leave the
aerials exactly in phase, and the paths on which they will be received in
phase form a family of hyperbolic lines originating between the Master and
each Slave. These 'in-phase' lines are the lines of the Decca Lattice. The
Decometers, which are in essence phase-meters, measure the exact phase-
difference, and so indicate zero on each in-phase line and some fractional
value when between the lines. They also count the number of complete
lanes and zones passed through.

Reproduced from *The Decca Navigator* and *The Decca Navigator System and
Its Uses*, by courtesy of The Decca Navigator Company Limited. London.

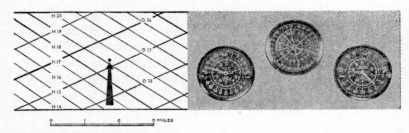

Two Decometers give the fix. The large hand points to Lane Numbers, the small to fractions of a lane, two places of decimals being readable. In the small square window a Zone Letter appears, indicating which group of lanes is being traversed.

When the ship's course is parallel to a lane the relevant Decometer pointer will remain stationary. Once every minute the Lane Identification Meter lights up and swings to the Lane Number of each Decometer in turn. Only the pointer inside the quadrant is read in Lane Identification. In the setting above, the Red Decometer indicates 19.2 in Zone H, Green 36.76 in Zone D, and the intersection of two lines on the chart corresponding to these values gives the exact position of the ship. The Lane Identification Meter confirms, momentarily, the Red Lane reading of 19.

Any vessel equipped with the Decca Navigator System becomes a receiving station for the wave patterns transmitted by the shore stations. A special receiver on the ship is tuned to pick up the signal patterns from the nearest Master station and its two most suitably situated Slave stations, each pair of which radiates a different frequency but with a common harmonic which is generated within the receiver. The dials of the receiver show a numerical value for each of the two wave patterns being received at the precise geographical position of the receiving station, that is the vessel herself, and her position can then be plotted on an ordinary navigational chart which has been specially overprinted with Decca lanes.

Within the limits of the areas covered by the Decca Navigator System, the position of a located wreck can be similarly and accurately recorded merely by noting the Decca co-ordinate readings at the instant the vessel passes over the wreck as indicated by the Echo Sounder trace. She is thus able to return to the exact position, time and time again, without the use of any visual marker. In fact, the Decca receiver is so sensitive

42

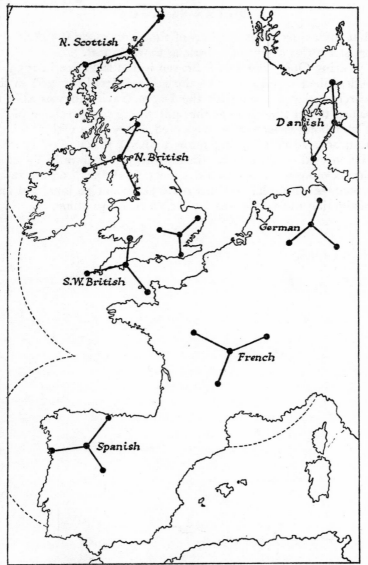

Part of the west European Coverage of the Decca Navigation System.
Within the area covered by this map, but not actually shown, there is now
a west Norwegian Chain which is linked with the N. Scottish Chain, and a
Frisian Islands Chain linking the German and Danish Chains.

From *The Decca Navigator* and by courtesy of The Decca Navigator Company
Limited. London.

that under perfect conditions of time and place the dials can register a movement of as little as fourteen feet.

During Operation Victor Search in the Irish Sea in 1959-60 —described in Chapter 11—the salvage vessel engaged in the search and equipped with the Decca Navigator was able to return to her moorings at the spot where the wreckage of the Victor bomber was being recovered, every time with unfailing accuracy. After steaming more than 35 miles from Milford Haven, with visibility sometimes down to less than half a mile, the six mooring buoys would appear dead ahead on the radar screen, relying solely on this remarkable navigational aid and navigating the whole way by Decca readings alone.

PART TWO

CHAPTER FOUR

NUESTRA SEÑORA

The Phips family was a large one—by any standard. Young William Phips had been preceded by twenty brothers and sisters, so it is doubtful whether he was brought up with any great luxury or had many favours bestowed upon him. His father, an armourer by trade, left Willie fatherless at the age of six but Mary Phips married again almost immediately and then proceeded to augment her already outsize family by presenting her youngest son William with five more brothers and sisters— a family which, one might think, may well have smothered any unusual characteristics which the young William might have otherwise developed, sandwiched as he was between such a mass of Phips's, five younger and twenty older, excluding his parents.

Times must have been very hard for the Phips family in the small village in Maine, on the north east coast of what is now the United States of America, where they were raised. James Phips, William's father, was an English Puritan who had gone to New England in the early part of the seventeenth century. Young William, probably, had little or no schooling and no doubt spent much of his boyhood helping to guard his father's sheep in the shore-side meadows of the village where they lived. Maybe it was here, within sight and sound of the sea, that the adventurer in him came to life.

In 1669, when he was just eighteen, William became apprenticed to a local naval shipyard and it was there, probably, that his imagination first became fired with colourful stories of pirates and treasure in the Spanish Main which must have been brought back by the crews of ships coming into the yard.

When he finished his apprenticeship four years later he was still unable to read or write, but went to Boston, married a merchant captain's daughter four years his senior, and then managed to borrow enough capital to return to his birthplace and establish his own shipyard. He was still only twenty-four years old but already setting foot on the ladder of success in spite of his lack of education. He was learning things the hard way, but learning them well and quickly.

The soaring profits of his shipyard provided enough finance to enable him to build his own ship, and this gave him the means of sampling the adventures of coastal trading for himself. The samples must have whetted his appetite for he rapidly acquired a vast amount of knowledge and experience. His voyages became longer and longer. During visits to the West Indies, stories of sunken treasure ships recreated his boyhood dreams and he also acquired, no doubt, much valuable information about some of the more promising wrecks and stored it in his memory for future reference.

He must have burned much midnight oil studying, too, for in the space of eight years he grew from an illiterate young man of twenty-two into a qualified engineer and navigator at the age of thirty. He was now moving towards bigger and more exciting undertakings. He made up his mind to go after treasure. His friends in Boston, however, were not very forthcoming and so, at the end of 1682, having failed to get the financial backing he required in Boston, he sailed for London. He needed more than his own modest coaster and limited resources to go treasure-hunting in the Spanish Main. Three hundred years later he would probably have floated a company and enticed people with more money than sense to provide the capital he required—but it was still only 1682. The Boston Puritans had not been interested, so William Phips turned his eyes as well as his little ship towards England, determined to meet none other than the popular, gay but dissolute King Charles II and to sell his project to him.

His project was not to be his only sale. On arrival in London
he sold his ship and then used the proceeds to buy for himself
the fancy clothes and wigs without which it would have been
impossible for him to move in Court circles. But move he did
and King Charles—much taken with this most adventurous
gentleman, his manner and his tales of wealth untold, just
waiting to be picked up and brought home—not only entered
into a sort of royal partnership but provided him with a fully
crewed 18-gun frigate. Knowing that the ship herself had been
captured from Algerian pirates must have added savour to the
venture for both partners.

King Charles, however, did not trust his new friend im-
plicitly. On board Phips's new command, the *Algier Rose*,
when he sailed for Boston on October 27th, 1682, was a Treasury
agent sent by the King to ensure that the treasure, if found,
came home and that the royal share was suitably large. The
relationship between this additional member of the crew and
Phips himself was, unfortunately far from harmonious and when
a rival captain with his own ship appeared on the scene in
Boston and demanded a joint expedition with any ensuing
treasure divided equally between the three of them, the
Treasury agent must have become suspicious—or perhaps he
feared for his life. Whatever the reason, he immediately set off
back to England, presumably to report to his royal master that
Mr. Phips was, in his opinion, up to no good.

With his partner's accredited representative on his way back
and therefore well out of the way, Phips hastened his preparations for starting the hunt. He recruited three young Indian
divers and, on January 19th, 1684, the two ships sailed for the
Great Bahamas Bank, that treacherous 300-mile long stretch
of water which lies between Cuba and the Bahama Islands,
strewn with coral reefs and hidden dangers, most of it covered
by less than ten, and nowhere by more than thirty, feet of water,
the graveyard of countless ships.

Phips knew where some of the more promising wrecks lay
and anchored as near one of them as he dared, but after several
days of intensive diving they found nothing except a few coins.
There were plenty more wrecks, and the naked Indian divers
were still keen enough. The two ships moved on. No weeks, or

47

even days, of fruitless searching in dark waters, hundreds of feet deep here. In these crystal clear and mostly shallow waters the remains of most of the wrecks could probably be seen, although the *Algier Rose* herself usually had to lay off in deeper water and send a boat in to locate the wreck.

His departure from Boston had been delayed more than he had anticipated and now Phips began to grow fearful of King Charles's agent returning to demand surrender of the ship and crew before he was able to show him some signs, at least, that his quest for treasure was something more than a wild goose chase. His crew, too, were growing restless. One day when the ship was at anchor in a bay on the sheltered side of a small uninhabited island so that the divers could scrape off some of the barnacles and weed which were rapidly making the *Algier Rose*'s sides below water look like an overgrown rock-garden, the greater part of the crew mutinied. Unfortunately for them, they chose to go on strike when they were ashore and were forced to surrender unconditionally when Phips ordered the faithful few remaining on board to hoist the anchor and head for the open sea. The strikers quickly decided that the *Algier Rose* was the lesser of two evils, the other one being an uninhabited desert island. They returned to the ship and surrendered their arms in return for an undertaking that they would be taken back to Jamaica and put ashore there. They had had their fill of treasure-hunting—without any treasure.

Port Royal, then also known as the Pirates' Capital, where they were landed, was no place to look for sea-going gentlemen to fill the recently vacated posts on the *Algier Rose*, and so Phips sailed for Puerto Plata on the north coast of Hispaniola, so named by Columbus when he first discovered the island in 1492 but now divided into the twin republics of Haiti and Santo Domingo. It was there, at Puerto Plata, that Phips found, not only his new men, but an old Spaniard who had information for sale; information which, to Phips, must have seemed a heaven-sent opportunity to fill his still empty treasure chests with the wherewithal to appease the Treasury Agent when he turned up again.

About forty years earlier, the flagship of the Spanish treasure fleet, a ship which bore the incongruous but quite beautiful name of *Nuestra Señora de la Concepcion*, had sailed from San Cristobal for Spain, her holds bursting with most of the previous years' proceeds of gold and silver which then flowed continuously from Mexico, the New Spain, to the treasuries of Spain herself. It was her last and most wandering voyage.

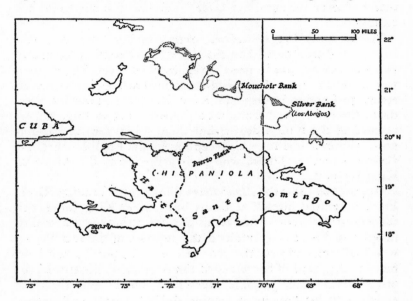

Her holds may have been bursting, metaphorically, at the seams with her treasure but they were, also, all but bursting literally, for her hull was sadly in need of extensive renovation. After many delays for temporary repairs to some of the older ships, including the *Nuestra Señora*, the fleet sailed. Twenty-four hours later eight ships out of the total of twenty were lost in a hurricane. The flagship survived—but only just. Damaged and partially dismasted, she was driven around at the mercy of wind and weather for almost a month and finally met her doom on the jagged foaming reefs of Los Abrojos, now called the Silver Bank, eighty miles north-north-east of Puerto Plata. Phips's latest casual acquaintance, the old Spaniard, was by a most extraordinary coincidence one of her few remaining survivors.

Here at last was the lucky break for which Phips had so long waited. In the spring of 1685 he set off once again. At the Bank, known then to the English as the Ambergris Bank—presumably a corruption of 'Abrojos' the *Algier Rose* anchored in safe waters while a boat, under the old Spaniard's directions, searched over the coral heads for the *Señora*; but she could not be found.

Weeks went by. Provisions were running low, the crew becoming discontented and the *Algier Rose* herself, after nearly two years away, was in need of repair. Now it was Phips's turn to choose the lesser of two evils, and his lesser evil now was to return to London to persuade King Charles to renew his overdraft. On calling at Bermuda on the way back to England, he learned of the King's death; but there was no turning round now, whatever might be his reception by the English court and Charles's brother James, who had succeeded to the throne as King James II.

August 1685 saw the *Algier Rose* sailing up the London River. Phips presented himself at Court but neither King James nor the Admiralty would listen to his plea for fitting out a new ship in spite of his having retained the support of Samuel Pepys, who had returned only the year before to the post he had held first in 1673, that of Secretary to the Admiralty. He turned his attention to other possible sources of finance but the year ended with his dreams of fortune sinking deeper and deeper into obscurity. Spring 1686 brought no corresponding upsurge into Phips's heart, but then his luck turned. In July he met again his benefactor of two years before, the Duke of Albemarle, who had introduced him to the court of King Charles in 1684 and who now pleaded on his behalf with the new King.

Now that he had returned to royal circles, rich friends who would have none of him before became interested again in the prospect of sharing his fortunes. With Treasury backing the Gentlemen Adventurers was formed with a working capital of £100, to which organization Phips offered his services as Director of Operations for a share of one sixteenth of the profits. Two ships were acquired; the *James & Mary* of 200 tons and the *Henry of London*, a smaller vessel of only 50 tons. Phips took over the *James & Mary* and no doubt regarded his new command as a good omen, bearing as it did the two royal names which happened to be also the names of his own father and mother.

The other shareholders of the company insured themselves against complete failure by insisting that the two ships took cargo out to the West Indies and returned loaded, too—if not with treasure then with some other, albeit less valuable, goods. Even if the company did not make a fortune, it would at least cover its outlay by having two cargoes of sugar, rum or tobacco to dispose of when the ships came back.

By December 1686, having discharged their cargoes, both vessels were in Puerto Plata preparing for their real mission. Although friendly relations had been established with the Spanish Governor, Phips had no wish for the real purpose of his visit to become known and so only the smaller ship, *Henry of London*, commanded by Phip's trusty ex-first officer of the *Algier Rose*, left Puerto Plata to reconnoitre. In a safe anchorage on the Ambergris Bank the *Henry of London* lay waiting while, day after day, a large ten-oared dug-out canoe which had been built in Puerto Plata without arousing suspicion and hidden below decks, set off to explore the dangerous waters in search of the *Nuestra Señora* and the fabulous treasure still held secret by her rotting timbers.

The New Year of 1687 dawned, but still the divers had found nothing. Every suspicious shape hidden by exotic corals and tropical marine growths which had been seen in the crystal clear waters had been probed, but always the canoe returned empty.

It was returning empty, too, one beautiful evening in February. The sun still shone from a brilliant sky, its rays striking obliquely through the transparent turquoise layer of sea which barely covered some of the coral reefs. A particularly colourful patch caught the eye of the officer in charge—maybe he thought a few branches would make a pretty necklace for someone he knew at home. Whatever the reason, he asked the diver to go down and get a piece for him. The glistening brown body streaked down through the clear water and remained there a few moments looking round for the best piece. The fan-shaped head he chose appeared to be growing on a rather unnatural-shaped lump of something, so he brought that up as well. That lump of something, when they had scraped away the coral, was a bar of silver. They had found the *Nuestra Señora*.

The spot was buoyed, and after only three days diving the *Henry of London* headed towards Puerto Plata with over 2,000 gold pieces, silver and gold ingots as well as other less valuable relics from the Spanish galleon, in her hold.

Phips was relieved to see the other ship return safely. He was delighted to find that she had not returned empty. The silver and gold, pottery and weapons that the divers had found held promise of greater prizes and both ships set off to the Ambergris Bank without delay. They anchored within sight of the buoy marking the spot where the divers had first picked up the silver bar encrusted with coral. The rest of it was probably much more than just encrusted, for in more than forty years it could have become buried under several feet of coral which, in some areas, grows at a prolific rate. Madrepores, a type of branching coral, on Tortuga Island off the coast of Venezuela, has been said to grow up to three inches in a year, while a reef off the north-east coast of Borneo was, at the end of the last century, reported to have become nineteen feet higher in thirty-two years—a growth of more than seven inches every twelve months.

But however much coral covered the gold and silver once carried by the *Nuestra Señora*, the divers reached at least some of it. On the evening of the first day's operations the divers brought back to the waiting ships about 240 coins, dollars and half dollars. That was on February 22nd, 1687. In the next eight weeks, by diving every day, they brought up by hand nearly 10 tons of ingots—some gold but the majority silver—and almost 13 tons of coin. With that cargo on board there was no question of returning, except to England; and as by then there were only enough provisions left on board to last such a voyage, both ships set sail for home.

The *James & Mary* was almost wrecked on the north-east part of the Mouchoir Bank reefs, about fifty miles to the westward, but she was spared the fate of becoming a second *Nuestra*, and the middle of May saw both vessels back in the

Thames—to a victorious welcome. The Admiralty, the Duke of Albemarle and, no doubt, King James himself were all highly delighted and the Gentlemen Adventurers were particularly anxious that the remainder of the hoard should not be lost. Help poured in. The Admiralty promised ships and an Admiral to go with them, and the Duke of Albemarle decided to honour the new mission with his own presence.

The Duke was not going just for a pleasure cruise, nor as a second Treasury Agent. He was, in fact, the new governor designate of the island of Jamaica. The post had been his for some time but he had not been in any hurry to take it up. Now, with a company of treasure hunters—in which he was certainly not completely disinterested—about to resume operations in the area, the Governorship suddenly became a much more pleasing proposition. Then, to add even more distinction to the campaign, the late commander of the *Algier Rose* was summoned to Windsor Castle and endowed with a knighthood. A few weeks later, Sir William Phips received the additional honour of the post of High Sheriff of Massachusetts.

The erstwhile village shepherd boy from Maine and once illiterate Boston shipyard apprentice had come a long way, and was now destined to return to his home country in high estate, for Maine was then a part of Massachusetts. It was not admitted to the Union as a separate state until the year 1820.

In September 1687 four ships sailed in company for the far off coral reefs and the rest of the treasure. There was the *Foresight* which wore the flag of the accompanying Admiral. Sir William Phips commanded one which bore a name more suited to an English country inn, the *Good Luck & a Boy*. The *Assistance* carried the Duke of Albemarle and the *Princess* completed the party. Phips's *Good Luck* did not live up to her name to start with, for she was damaged by a storm in the Channel and was forced to return to London for repairs. The other ships waited several weeks on the north coast of Hispaniola for her to rejoin them.

At last the convoy set off for the wreck but other adventurous gentlemen must have heard about the submarine Aladdin's cave for, when they arrived, they found several other ships there already in the area. However, the four British ships in company, one with an Admiral and another with a Duke on board must have made some impression on the would-be poachers, for they soon made off, and operations began. But the divers soon found that it was not so much 'would-be' as 'had been'. In the seven months since the *Algier Rose* had left the scene most of the recoverable treasure had disappeared.

By the following May all that could be found had been brought up. True, it was more than just a little. In bullion and specie it totalled over five tons, but much remained down below. So far, the interior of the hull had not been penetrated but this was a task beyond the resources of naked divers working only with their hands. Blasting gelignite for opening up wrecks was still to come, and a diver who depended on the capacity of his lungs alone to enable him to stay under water was no substitute. Phips wanted desperately to be able to break right into the wreck but the means to achieve that end were beyond him, and he was forced to give up. The campaign was over, and the ships went their ways. The Duke of Albemarle went to his appointment in Jamaica and the *Good Luck & a Boy* carried the new High Sheriff back to Massachusetts, back to his home and his family; back, perhaps, to a less adventurous life than he had led over the previous six years, but his achievement had not been insignificant. Without the help of any diving appliances or mechanical aids he had carried out the first great treasure-salvage operation and had succeeded in recovering gold and silver bullion and specie to the value of £300,000. In those days that was a vast enough sum. Today, even if only one tenth of the total weight was gold and the remainder silver, it would be worth upwards of £2,000,000.

Four years later, in 1682, when Sir William was only forty-one years old, he became Governor of Massachusetts. Now, surely, he was at the top of the ladder he had started, so precariously, to climb in 1675 but Fate, having raised him so high, intervened once more. In 1692 he died suddenly whilst visiting London and was buried in the old church of St. Mary Woolnoth in Lombard Street.

More than one attempt has been made since to find the wreck of the *Nuestra Señora de la Concepcion*. The most recent one was

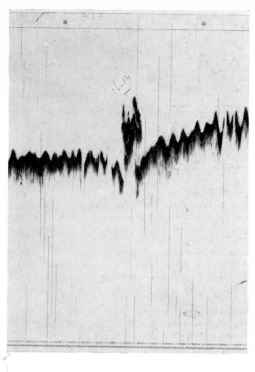

Plate 5*a*,
Echo sounder record
of small wreck

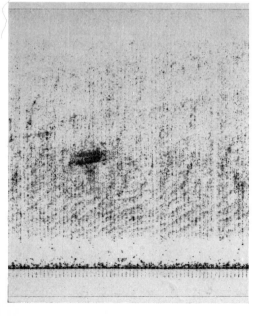

Plate 5*b*,
Transit sonar record
of same wreck

Plate 6, The *Laurentic*

beset with bad luck and even worse weather and never really cleared the English Channel.

Perhaps the coral has claimed its own for ever or, perhaps, 'Finis' has yet to be written to the story of the ship with the holy name.

CHAPTER FIVE

TOBERMORY

In the year 1583 King Philip of Spain was annoyed. His Admiral, the Marques de Santa Cruz was also annoyed.

That their annoyance should still be having repercussions in Tobermory Bay in Argyllshire nearly 400 years later seems an absurd suggestion, though in fact it holds more than a modicum of truth: if the King and his Admiral had not been annoyed, there might not have been any stories of a Spanish treasure galleon being at the bottom of Tobermory Bay. One could go further and put all the blame on to the poor sailors.

The seamen adventurers of Queen Elizabeth 1 of England had been rather unfriendly towards the Spaniards in the West Indies, especially where treasure was concerned, and King Philip was persuaded by his Admiral to seek his revenge by sending the Armada to conquer England. The Admiral died while the great fleet was assembling in the port of Lisbon.

It was an impressive gathering—one hundred and thirty ships, many of them over 700 tons, and a miscellaneous collection of sailors, soldiers and slaves totalling some 24,000 men. It was, however, no Spithead Review. Spain, at that time, had no Royal Navy and both vessels and men had been collected from all over the Spanish Empire—a motley company.

They sailed on May 18th, 1588, but some soon fell victims to bad weather, bad water, bad food or all three, and put into La Coruña on the north coast of Spain on June 9th. Their troubles had started. They were there for several weeks while others sailed on and then waited for the stragglers to rejoin them. Off the Isles of Scilly they had a grand rendezvous, formed up into a giant crescent like a new moon, seven miles from point to point, and sailed majestically into the English Channel where they were first seen off the Lizard Head on July 19th.

The English fleet was in the Channel, too, but not all in one place. Sir Francis Drake had about ninety armed merchant ships at Plymouth. The rest, under Lord Henry Seymour, were in the Downs, at the other end of the English Channel. The Armada was, in fact, bound for the Straits of Dover; waiting for them in Flanders, under the Duke of Parma, was a large army with which the Armada was supposed to effect the invasion of England.

The total English fleet numbered one hundred and ninety-seven, but many of the ships were small and of little use against the Spanish galleons, and this rather offset the numerical superiority of the English.

Lord Howard of Effingham took the Plymouth ships out and harassed the Spaniards in a running encounter which lasted over two days. A second engagement took place off Portland on July 23rd and another off the Isle of Wight, and on the 28th the Spanish fleet, now through the Dover Strait and in Calais Roads, came up against the entire English fleet, the two parts of which had now joined.

That night the curtain rose on the first act of the disastrous play which was to end with the almost complete destruction of the crown of Spanish maritime glory. The Armada lay peacefully at anchor, with the English still then at a safe distance—or so they thought. Under cover of darkness, Lord Howard manœuvred some of his older ships to windward of the Spaniards, set them on fire and sailed them, unmanned, right into the sleeping Armada. Utter panic broke out as the galleons struggled to free themselves from their uninvited, unexpected, fiery visitors. With no time to weigh anchor, most of the galleons simply cut their cables and made off as best they could with the English ships following. Sixteen of the Spanish galleons were only just saved from being cut off and taken as prizes by a sudden freshening of the wind which drove them to leeward. This also had the effect of virtually halting the battle.

The ill wind was already preparing to live up to its reputation of not being so ill that it was not blowing good to somebody. By the 29th, off Gravelines, ten miles farther east, the Spaniards were in full flight, driven as much by the wind as by the English, who were by now beginning to scrape the bottoms of their ammunition lockers.

July 30th dawned with the Spanish fleet well past Nieuport, another twenty-five miles farther away from the invasion of England. Already nine ships had been lost. Their proud seven-mile crescent of sail was now no more, and with less than thirty feet of water underneath them, driven closer and closer to the shore and with the English still to windward, their doom must have seemed barely over the horizon. It was now that the ill wind became less ill for the Spaniards, and backed to the south-west. It was their salvation. They turned and ran northwards, scattering as they went and with the English hard on their heels.

Off the Firth of Forth, on August 13th, Lord Howard gave up the chase. Although the Armada was far from destroyed—there were still nearly one hundred ships fleeing to the north—the English Lord High Admiral knew that they could no longer have any intention of making their way back to the English Channel. The Spaniards' only way home now was to keep going, round the north of Scotland and then down the west coast. Eventually fifty-four ships out of the original one hundred and thirty reached home waters. Out of the nineteen lost or wrecked on the way round, one left its remains in Tobermory Bay.

That one of the ships of the Spanish Armada did get as far as, but no farther than, this bay on the north-east coast of the island of Mull in Scotland seems fairly certain. Whether she really was the treasure ship of the Armada, the *Almirante de Florencia*, laden with gold, jewels and Spanish doubloons worth altogether about £2,000,000 is, to say the least of it, shrouded in uncertainty.

The story has it that she was blown up while at anchor in Tobermory Bay. Previously the Spaniards had gone ashore and captured a Highland Chieftain, one Donald McLean, and held him prisoner on the ship. He found his way into the galleon's magazine after dark one night and, preceding Guy Fawkes futile efforts by seventeen years, successfully sent himself and five hundred men still on board sky high—and the ship to the bottom.

The seventh Duke of Argyll, however, certainly did hear about a Spanish galleon being sunk in the Bay from one Andres Pereira who was ashore with some of the galleon's soldiers at the time of the disaster, and he decided to put his knowledge to good advantage. The Argylls had raised troops for King Charles I's Irish wrangles, for which the account rendered was for the sum of £40,000. In settlement of this debt, the Duke accepted the wreck, and wealth if any, of the Spanish ship 'and any other wrecks cast away on the shores and in the waters of Mull'; and so the successive Dukes of Argyll have had, and still have, a wreck dating from 1588 in Tobermory Bay. The *Almirante de Florencia*? Who knows. The Spaniards are supposed to have listed the *Almirante* among those that got away and struggled back to Spain and said that, in any case, she was no treasure ship.

So what of the wreck which does, or did, lie in Tobermory Bay? Certainly a Spanish ship was sunk there, for things have been recovered which undoubtedly had their origin in Spain at about the right time for it to have belonged to the Armada.

In 1665, the wreck was supposed to have been inspected from a diving bell and between 1680 and 1683 one Archibald Miller of Greenock is said to have actually worked on it, and lifted guns and anchors. Whatever truth there is in this, there certainly is, in Inveraray Castle, the ancestral home of the Dukes of Argyll, a great bronze demi-culverin—a 4·5-inch calibre gun of the sixteenth century which weighs 3,000 lb. and threw a 9¼ lb. shot a distance of '2,500 paces'. On the touch hole of the gun at Inveraray, a gun which was salvaged from Tobermory Bay before 1720, there is the cypher of the great Italian artificer Benvenuto Cellini who was born in Florence in 1500. So there *is* something at the bottom of Tobermory Bay which could have sunk there in 1588.

Much later, but some time before 1912, a Colonel Foss worked on the site of the wreck with a primitive form of air-lift and succeeded in bringing up a number of most interesting relics including some plate, coins and a pair of dividers. His operations also resulted in the meeting of two very old friends—for he found the twin of the great bronze demi-culverin. It joined the collection at Inveraray Castle which now includes a pewter dish—a dish which appeared to be an ordinary enough piece of débris when it was fished up in the Bay. But in 1950, when it was cleaned by the British Museum, it revealed the arms of none other than Andres Pereira.

In the same year that the identity of the pewter dish was established, the Admiralty offered to undertake an 'on site' investigation, presumably as an exercise for their divers. Now, at long last, with experts on the job, some part of this mythical treasure would see the light of day. They came, they exercised, and they went, without having recovered any gold or jewels or even a gun or two—nor yet another pewter dish. Nothing yet proved the existence or otherwise of a Spanish treasure ship 'cast away on the shores or in the waters of Mull'.

Two years later, the present Duke of Argyll himself took to digging holes where the Royal Navy had exercised their divers. To be precise, he did not dig but sucked out a hole, twenty feet deep, with an eight-inch air-lift. Apart from some pieces of timber, this operation yielded nothing of particular value, but the Duke did not despair. The following year, with the help of a Tank Landing Craft and a five-ton grab, he dug a couple of trenches twenty feet deep where the wreck was believed to be. All the excavated material was dumped on to the tank deck where the silt was washed away with a hose. What would not wash away was quite impressive.

There were pottery oil jars, glassware, a lot of deck planking and a five-foot long brass cannon—a cannon which was proved by an inscribed signature and date to have been cast in Italy in 1559, twenty-nine years before the Armada sailed for England.

Even more recently, in 1865, and again in 1967, an attempt was made, using the latest detection devices, to solve the mystery of some hard lumps down below the harbour bed and under sixty feet of water—and another twenty feet of clay silt. Previously, it was thought that these buried 'high points' might have been ship's ballast. Not any ship's but a Spanish Armada ship's ballast—if wishful thinking was to carry any weight. The 1967 investigation proved their existence but also their local connections. They were stone dumpings left over from the building of Tobermory pier.

When, in 1950, the Naval divers finished exercising in Tobermory Bay without proving the existence or otherwise of the Spanish Armada treasure ship, they went away—but not quite empty-handed. At least, they were not empty-handed when they finished exercising although they were when they actually left. They had, unfortunately, lost the button they had found in the harbour but, on the other hand, they had managed to photograph it before it was lost. That was indeed fortunate for how else could it have been proved that it too bore the arm of Andres Pereira?

The photograph—which was supposed to be of this button recovered from the wrecked straggler of the great Spanish invasion fleet nearly four hundred years before—did not, however, link the interesting object with Andres Pereira. Instead it was said to have been identified as belonging to a Tobermory housemaid's dressing gown; but, of course, it might have been four hundred years old and the housemaid might have had a secret meeting with Andres. The button might have been a keepsake which he lost in the harbour. So, perhaps, there was some connection—or perhaps not.

CHAPTER SIX

THE *LAURENTIC*

In the First World War, the 14,892-ton White Star liner *Laurentic* was taken over by the Admiralty and converted to an armed merchant cruiser. She thus became His Majesty's ship *Laurentic* and it was in this capacity that she sailed for Halifax, Nova Scotia in January 1917. Included in her cargo were 40 tons of gold to pay for munitions and supplies for Britain and her allies. (Plate 6.)

The two main sea routes to and from British ports, the English Channel and north of Ireland, were both full of lurking death from enemy submarines and mines and it was to one of these that the *Laurentic* fell victim. Before she had cleared Northern Ireland she struck a mine and sank off Lough Swilly on January 25th, 1917. She took with her, to the bottom, over five million pounds worth of gold bullion.

This vast wealth could not be allowed to end its days where it was, lying imprisoned in a wreck on the sea bed in 120 feet of water. It was vital to Britain's war effort that its purchasing power should be used, and used soon. War or no war, it had to be recovered, and salvage operations were put in hand by the Admiralty almost at once. In charge was Captain G. C. C. Damant, C.B.E., R.N. (retired).

The salvage vessel had little difficulty in finding the wreck for the *Laurentic* had gone down only two miles or so from Fanad Point. The depth of water over the ship was about 60 feet, which was well within the limits of soft suit diving and so, unlike other famous salvage operations to come the necessary explosive charges for blasting open the wreck could be placed by hand. There would be no tedious and frustrating hours trying to drop the charges, dangling at the end of hundreds of feet of wire rope, on to the right spot. When they got through to the bullion, the divers would be able to pick up the gold bars with their own hands.

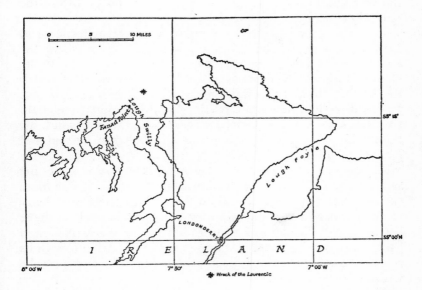

A diver's survey showed that the *Laurentic* was lying on her port bilge with a 60 degree list. Half-way down her starboard, and therefore upper, side there was a pair of watertight doors designed to give access to the baggage room containing the gold. All they had to do was to open the doors, walk into the baggage room and pick up the gold. It was not quite so easy as that, of course. The angles of both deck and ship's side were such that the divers could not stand or walk on either; but in spite of this difficulty, when salvage operations started a few months after the sinking it did not seem, then, that it would be many more months before the bulk of the gold was back on dry land.

63

At first, when German submarines were still doing their utmost to interrupt the vital flow of shipping, both inward and outward, mines in the area presented a constant danger to the salvage vessel in her journeyings to and from the wreck, but minesweepers kept the way clear for her—as well as keeping the minelaying submarines busy laying more. By far the biggest menace of all was the weather, not only in the vicinity but hundreds of miles to the westward as well; and as it turned out the war was to finish and six years of peace go by before the operation was brought to a close.

Everything bad as far as weather is concerned comes to Britain from across the Atlantic ocean and, from where the *Laurentic* went down, one can see an awful lot of that. From the coast of Iceland 600 miles away to the north-west, southwards to Newfoundland 1,700 miles away, there is unbroken ocean. In one direction, between Greenland and Labrador, one could travel in a straight line for 1,900 miles before striking land. To the south-west, there is 4,000 miles of sea between Ireland and the West Indies.

Although, therefore, the position of the wreck gave the salvage vessel adequate protection from the south it was more than exposed to bad weather from the west, for there was plenty of open water in that direction for the Atlantic swell to make itself felt. Nor did the bad weather have to be there, off Lough Swilly. It could be hundreds of miles out in the Atlantic with its resultant swell rolling in past Northern Ireland—and over the wreck of the *Laurentic*.

Although it is the wave or undulation, and not the water itself, which moves across the ocean surface, the horizontal movement of the undulation does cause each particle of water affected by the wave to move in a circular orbit. The diameter of this orbit is equal to the height of the wave from trough to crest. This circular movement continues downward through the water but becomes progressively smaller until, at a depth equal to half the length of the waves from crest to crest, it ceases altogether at a level known as the wave base. At any one level down to the wave base this circular movement creates a horizontal surge alternating in opposite directions, so that a swell with a wave height of 20 feet, a wave length of 250 feet and a resultant wave base at 125 feet would cause a slight surge, even right on the sea bed, at 120 feet where the *Laurentic* lay. Immediately above the wreck the movement would be considerable and such conditions caused many delays and gave the divers many uncomfortable, dangerous and frightening moments.

After the initial survey, the position of the ship's doors was marked with a buoy and moorings shifted so that the salvage vessel could remain right over the spot where the divers were to work. The first task was to remove or open the doors.

When the *Laurentic*'s boats were lowered before she sank, the rope falls with heavy three-sheaved blocks on the ends were left hanging from the davits, then about 60 feet above the water. On the high side of the wreck, the davit heads with the falls hanging from them were not much more than 60 feet below the surface so that a swell with a wave length of only 150 feet was sufficient to cause a surge which set all the boat falls swinging to and fro like so many pendulums. This made it necessary for the divers, when they were not dodging the swinging falls, to hang on to something for most of the time whenever there was a moderate swell running; they could move about only in the few brief moments between the surge one way and its reverse movement in the opposite direction.

The first explosive charges almost completely removed the two heavy doors in the ship's side. After they had been cleared out of the way, the next diver to go down found his passage barred by an iron grille gate and this also was removed without difficulty by blasting. Two hours later the door of the baggage room itself had been prised open—and the diver found himself sitting on top of a pile of gold, the whole five million pounds worth. It was packed in boxes about 12 inches square and 6 inches deep, four bars to a box; but the boxes weighed about 140 lb. each and, although this would have been only a little over 100 lb. under water, carrying a box out of the baggage room and up the steep passage to the opening in the ship's side was not an easy job. Still, the nature of the boxes' contents and the knowledge that each one was worth about £8,000 at that time, probably made the task a little less difficult, and the first box was recovered before the day had ended.

Next morning, three more were carried out of the steel

treasure chest and hoisted aboard; but before anything further was achieved a fierce northerly gale, which blew up suddenly, forced the salvage ship to seek shelter in harbour, and kept her there for a couple of weeks. During the gale, much of the coast there became littered with wreckage and, by the time the weather had moderated sufficiently for them to go out again, they had begun to fear the worst. The moorings had been damaged and had to be relaid, but the first look at the wreck confirmed the very worst of their forebodings. The wreck was no longer a wreck in name only. Under the strain of the terrific surge set up by the gale-swept sea above, the ship had folded up, like a partly-flattened out bottle carton. The door opening was still there on the upper side but it was 40 feet deeper than before and now only 20 feet above the surrounding sea bed.

Inside the opening, what had been a clear passage between decks only a few weeks before was now a narrow gap barely 18 inches high and filled with crumpled steel. The enemy had succeeded in sending the gold to the bottom but the weather had proved to be an even worse enemy and the gold was now well and truly buried. By blasting away the crumpled steelwork and shoring up as they went, divers eventually reached the bullion room for the second time but, like Old Mother Hubbard, when they got there the cupboard was bare. Not only bare but split wide open across the floor. The empty and twisted 'cupboard' was now about 120 feet down, level with the surrounding sea bed into which, of course, the wreck had now partially sunk.

When the ship collapsed under the relentless pressure and surge of the water, the boxes of gold must have gone down through the now open floor and slided away into whatever spaces still remained below. From the state of the wreck and the general angle of the crushed decks below the bullion room, they could do no more than surmise where the precious boxes might then be lying and, after calculating the most likely position of the gold in the chaos of steel decks and partitions, they embarked on the stupendous task of blasting a way downwards from a place on the now crumpled ship's side and vertically above where the gold was estimated to be.

This dangerous operation—made even more dangerous

because settlement of the wreck, accompanied by frightening noises and tremors, was still taking place—necessitated the divers crawling through narrow openings between buckled plates in complete darkness. Their peace of mind, if they managed to retain any, was further disturbed by shock waves from mines being exploded by sweepers in the channel only a few miles away—so much so that it was decided to stop operations entirely whenever minesweepers were working within five miles.

The farther they went down into the tangled mass, the more smashed cabin furniture and fittings and other wreckage had to be pulled out of the way, mostly by hand, but at last their brave efforts were rewarded. Two months after resumption of operations they found gold again. By September over 130 boxes had been retrieved and then work was stopped for the winter. Bad weather came in early that first year, and it was obvious that suitable diving days were going to be few and far between from then on.

As it turned out, it was to be more than a year before they returned. Other operational commitments prevented the team from resuming until after the end of the war and it was spring 1919 before anyone again saw the wreck of the *Laurentic*. Knowing what a few weeks' gales had done in 1917 they were amazed to find that the crumpled ship was no more crumpled than when they left her eighteen months before. After clearing away débris and more than a year's accumulation of sand and mud, gold was once more uncovered and, box by box, carried out and hoisted aboard the salvage vessel.

Towards the end of the 1919 operations it became apparent that they had found only one part of all the gold which had slipped through the broken floor of the bullion room. Bars and boxes were getting fewer and fewer. They were faced also with the possibility of having to demolish some of the superstructure which, on both sides of their 'hole', had not collapsed as much as the section around the bullion room. By the time that season ended, the jagged overhanging structure above presented a frightening picture to the divers as they descended into dark tunnels in search of their ever diminishing treasure, but so long as each day yielded a few more boxes or even stray shining bars nobody wanted to stop and take to cutting and blasting again. So, with the next winter already poking its ugly head round the corner, they called a halt once more and counted the season's harvest. A further 300 bars had been found, bringing the total value recovered to over £1,250,000.

When they resumed work, in the spring of 1920, they found that their seasonal enemy, bad weather, had not only demolished much of the superstructure for them while they had been away—which was a kindly act—and then spoiled it all by shovelling the lot into their hole, but had taken care to see that the excavation was first filled with rubble and reinforced concrete. At least, it could not have been worse if someone had done just that. Tons of gravel and mud, swept into the bottom of the wreck by the combined effects of tides and storm surge, and now mixed up with débris from inside the wrecked superstructure—smashed cabin furniture, splintered deck planking and so on—had formed into a solid mass, which was now covered over with plating from the collapsed upperworks. Their clock had been put back for two whole years and it took them two more to put it right.

Right through the working seasons of 1920 and 1921 they blasted, cleared, dug, blasted and cleared away, again and again, and had it not been for an odd bar or two of gold appearing occasionally, hope would surely have died as the long, frustrating days wore on. As it was, the total wages for those two years of labour was 50 pieces of gold.

By the time that 1921 season ended it was clear, from the particular parts of the ship that were then being uncovered, that they were right through to the bottom of the wreck itself. With what forebodings they returned in the spring of 1922 can well be imagined. Had the gremlins been away for that winter, too, or had their 'fillers-in' been at work again? They were soon to know.

Yes, the gremlins had been there, after all, but with brooms instead of shovels. Some of the silt had been actually washed away in their absence and when the first diver reached the bottom of what, by then, was more like a gap between two wrecks than a hole in one, he saw bars of gold protruding from the sand. Not many boxes had remained whole after the bullion room had been emptied, and for some time single bars had outnumbered boxes. From then on it was a matter of almost 'panning' for gold. On that very first day of operations in 1922, nineteen bars were dug up. Digging, scraping, feeling, picking out, then scraping again went on day after day, until an area of nearly 440 square feet inside the bottom of the wreck had been picked clean and almost completely cleared.

They were tracking the gold now like following the trail in a paper chase, one bar leading to the discovery of another. At one stage the trail led away beneath layers of crushed plating which had to be blasted away, and then there was more tunnelling. Under there the shell plating, folded like corrugated iron, bore witness to the tremendous force of that underwater surge. Each valley in the plating was filled with sand and this gave the diver, feeling ahead with his hands and in almost complete darkness, the uncanny sensation of having reached the edge of the world—or, at any rate, the edge of the plate.

Light does not penetrate very far in coastal waters, especially during out-going tides when the dirty water from rivers is being carried away. In the clear waters of the open ocean the different light waves are absorbed at different depths, and although the blue light of the spectrum may penetrate to a depth of between 400 and 800 feet, the yellow/green light to which the human eye mostly responds starts fading away about 300 feet down. Where the *Laurentic* was lying, divers in the 'open' could sometimes see as far as 20 feet, but much of the time at this stage they were like moles tunnelling under the ground and depended as much on feeling as seeing—and feeling for gold had to be learned. It took about six months for the divers to become really adept at that and a new diver, inexperienced in digging for gold, sometimes used up a lot of energy and enthusiasm extricating a hard, smooth piece of 'something' from under a foot or so of sand, only to find that it was a piece of broken wash basin or lavatory pan.

These sand-filled valleys, however, produced their quota of gold including some which also bore witness to the relentless power of moving water. Some of the bars recovered during this latter period were embedded with pebbles or heads of rivets;

others were twisted and squeezed as if they had been made of plasticine and some were bent almost double.

In the seven operational months of the 1922 season a further 940 bars were scooped, hosed and dug out of the sand and pebbles and shingle which accumulated again almost as fast as it could be removed. One cannot shovel sand away under water for as soon as the shovelful is lifted or moved, the sand just drops off the shovel and returns whence it came. Sacks with steel scoops fitted in the mouths, in conjunction with high pressure hoses and bare hands, were the tools with which the divers hunted their elusive quarry—working in overlapping relays so that both divers were down together for about four minutes to help each other with the filled sacks.

Each diver stayed down for only half an hour, but his ascent was spread over an additional thirty minutes, with stops at 30, 20 and 10 feet to allow for a controlled decompression. A regular relay of divers with half-hour working periods on the bottom was the most economical way of using these valuable men, for a further ten minutes work at that depth would have necessitated additional and longer stops and added twenty minutes to the ascent time.

The bags of excavated sand and shingle had to be pulled out and dumped clear of the area where they were working, but in spite of this everlasting fight against the sea bed itself coming back into its own the value of that 1922 season's crop was no less than £1,500,000, the 'pickings' of one record day having totalled 94 bars.

Their hunting tactics proved highly successful. By the time the 1923 season ended only 154 bars out of the original consignment of 3,211 remained unaccounted for, and that year's return alone was nearly £2,000,000.

The spring and summer of 1924 took compassion on them and their six long years of struggle, and the weather was kind. The cleared area of 440 square feet was increased to 2,000 square feet and gave up 129 of the last remaining 154 bars. Their best year, 1923, had no less than 1,255 bars to its credit. The worst, the year following the collapse of the wreck, yielded only seven.

Less than one per cent of the original treasure had eluded its

Plate 7a
Bow of the *Seydlitz*

Plate 7b,
Stern of the *Bayern*
showing airlocks

Plate 8a,
Bottom of the *Prinzregent Luitpold* showing airlocks

Plate 8b,
Prinzregent Luitpold passing under Forth Bridge

hunters who had come right through the seven years—and one of the most dangerous salvage operations ever attempted—absolutely unscathed. There had not been even one serious accident, and that alone was a great tribute to Captain Damant and his team.

CHAPTER SEVEN

SCAPA FLOW

The Great War was over. Twenty-one years later, when the second holocaust burst upon Europe, it became the First World War but then, in 1918, it was still the Great War.

Ten days had passed since the Armistice brought the four

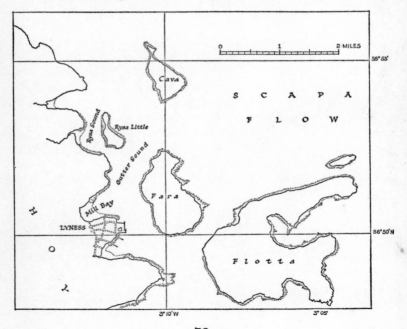

years' slaughter to an end and, below the Forth Bridge, the German High Seas Fleet was surrendering to Admiral Beatty. It was November 21st, 1918.

All the German submarines had gone into Harwich and while Great Britain and her allies argued what to do with them and the 10 Battleships, 6 Battle Cruisers, 8 Light Cruisers and nearly 50 Destroyers, the whole of this surface fleet, in charge of Admiral Ludwig von Reuter, retired into ignominious internment in Scapa Flow, north-east of the island of Hoy in the Orkney Islands.

The long dark winter passed into spring, spring gave way to summer, and the anchored German fleet became almost as much a part of the local scenery as were the smaller islands of Rysa Little, Cava and Fara round which the ships lay.

On the morning of June 21st, 1919, the First Battle Squadron of the British Fleet, and its attendant destroyers left Scapa Flow on exercise. Remaining in the Flow was one destroyer on duty, two under repair, one depot ship and a few drifters and trawlers. For the first time that year, Scapa Flow was almost completely deserted, apart from its more permanent 'local scenery'.

Something else unusual happened on that calm summer day. By the time the British ships returned in the afternoon, half of that 'local scenery' was on the bottom or in process of getting there. While the British Lions had been out for an airing, the whole German fleet had been scuttled by its own crews.

Some of the destroyers were saved from being totally wrecked. Four were prevented from sinking by British boarding parties and eighteen others were beached on the nearby islands. All of the remainder went to the bottom and thereby became the subject of the largest, longest and one of the most expensive salvage operations ever undertaken. It lasted 15 years and involved the raising of no fewer than 25 destroyers and 13 capital ships, seven of which had completely turned turtle and were bottom up.

It all started with a Mr. Ernest Frank Guelph Cox—who had turned to breaking up ships after the 1914–18 war—buying an ex-German floating dock from the Admiralty. This had a lifting capacity of 3,000 tons, and together with a large amount of merchant shipping, had been taken over after the war as reparations—but it was no ordinary dry dock. On its floor was a huge steel cylinder 40 feet across and 400 feet long, designed for testing submarines. Not that Ernest Cox wanted to become a submarine tester but he did have an eye for valuable scrap, and the cylinder promised to be just that. It was one of the partners in a Danish firm, which purchased a good deal of his scrap metal, who suggested to him that, after he had realized on the submarine-testing cylinder, the dock might be worth far more than its own value as scrap if it was used to raise some of the ex-German destroyers in Scapa Flow.

He took to the idea, called on the Admiralty and told them he wanted to buy some of those wrecks up in Scapa Flow. Their Lordships were a little sceptical and suggested that he first went and had a look at what he proposed buying. He went, he saw and—after making history by buying possibly the first ever first-class season ticket between Thurso and London—he purchased. When he left the Admiralty for the second time he did so as the new and proud owner of 26 destroyers and a couple of battleships lying on the bottom in Scapa Flow.

Ernest Cox planned to convert his huge U-shaped floating dock into two 200-foot long L-shaped sections, but for the 700-mile eight-day tow up to Lyness in the Orkneys he merely removed one of the side walls, thus leaving himself with a full-length L-shaped dock. It made its voyage north, from Queensborough in the Thames estuary, with its long floor piled high with every conceivable variety of salvage equipment as well as railway lines, trucks and a couple of crane jibs. The side wall, already containing some of the various workshops and machinery of an ordinary floating dock, had been adapted to include generators and compressors and the rest of the paraphernalia required for its new role.

It was beached at Mill Bay near Lyness, and then cut in two to make two 200-foot long L shapes. Each section was then fitted with a system of winches and pulley blocks for lifting the ships—by hand. On each half dock there were 12 sets of lifting gear and each set comprised a 3-gear hand winch and two 100-ton 5-sheaved pulley blocks.

The 750-ton destroyer V.70 was only half a mile from Cox's

base at Lyness. She was upright, in 50 feet of water, and presented an obvious first choice. Another first choice was to use chains instead of the more usual wire ropes for the actual lifting. Cox already had a vast quantity of anchors and anchor cables from his shipbreaking activities and as he had already spent about £40,000 on additional equipment he was not anxious to add to this by purchasing great lengths of new 9-inch circumference steel-wire rope.

The two half docks were towed out and anchored, one on either side of the sunken destroyer. It was March, 1924. The first choice of the V.70 did not prove unwise, but the first choice of chain cable for lifting, unfortunately, did.

In Scapa Flow there is a tidal range of 10 feet at spring tides. Under such conditions, if the lifting wires or chains were tightened up at low water, the tidal lift would result in the wreck being 10 feet off the bottom at high water without any actual lifting being done by the winches. The sunken vessel could then be moved into shallower water until she grounded and the same process repeated as often as necessary. Greater lift could be obtained by continuing to raise the vessel mechanically until shortly before high water, provided sufficient time was left for her to be moved inshore before the tide began to fall. This was the method generally adopted throughout the operations on the destroyers.

As the V.70 was upright, they were able to raise her stern sufficiently—by means of wires under the propeller shafts—to get all the lifting chains into position underneath the hull without much difficulty. In ten days everything was ready, and 'Lifting Day' dawned with all the promise of a fine calm day ahead. Just before the tide started rising the 24 teams of winchmen—four men to each winch—tightened up the chains so that all bore an equal strain and then began lifting. Both docks heeled inwards with the growing weight and then stopped, indicating that the V.70 was being lifted clear of the bottom. The March day was continuing fine but suddenly it was no longer calm—except in the meteorological sense. One of the 3-inch chains parted, throwing extra strain on the others which gave way, in turn, one after the other. Within seconds, broken chain cable and other parts of the lifting gear were flying in all

75

directions but everyone, miraculously, escaped injury. That was the beginning, and the end, of using old ships' anchor cables for lifting the Scapa Flow wrecks, and the chains were replaced by 9-inch circumference steel-wire rope with a breaking strain of 250 tons.

The delivery of the new wire rope in April marked the beginning of another three months of preparation for the second attempt. Wire slings were cut and spliced and then the lifting wires had to be passed underneath the hull of the V.70 which had, fortunately, fallen back into her former upright position when the chains parted at the first attempt. By the end of July, all twelve lifting wires were in position and 'Lifting Day II' also dawned fine and calm.

It was 4 a.m. on July 31st, 1924, and low water, when the 96-strong winch party manned the 24 winches and commenced winching. This time everything held and all went without a hitch. The men turned, the winch barrels slowly revolved, the lifting wires came in inch by inch and the V.70 rose from her bed of mud. They went on winding right up to near high water by which time the whole of the destroyer's upperworks were showing above the surface.

It was the first time the bridge of the V.70 had been dry for more than five years, but those years had not been entirely wasted. Nature's painters had, apparently, been extremely busy and had transformed the dull, grey, dead instrument of war into a fantastic array of coloured marine growth, animal as well as vegetable. Others, too, had been busy during those years of internment. Others, who shall be nameless, with an eye for valuable scrap—an eye as keen as Ernest Cox's own—and blessed with more than average pluck and healthy lungs, had succeeded in removing most of what was saleable and accessible, including the V.70's torpedo tubes which were constructed of gun metal and worth about £100 each.

As none of this valuable material could have been openly disposed of as 'Genuine—guaranteed removed from scuttled German fleet in Scapa Flow', it is more than possible that the larger items were cut up and sent to the mainland in boxes which bore a remarkable similarity to herring boxes, and smelled strongly of fish. But nobody ever really knew—or, if they did, they all appeared to suffer from a chronic loss of memory.

If the V.70 looked very beautiful when she first came out, her beauty was only fish deep. By the time she was beached at Mill Bay four tidal lifts later, the jellyfish and anemones and shell fish and all the rest of the marine growth with which she was adorned was dead, and stinking to high heaven. The smell was a fitting prelude to a most unkind twist of fate. After only just surviving a night's howling gale while under tow, slung between the twin half docks, on the way in to Lyness after the last beaching; and after giving everyone a most uncomfortable and frightening night, the triumphant salvors were temporarily shattered to learn that the price of their kind of scrap had suffered a disastrous slump. While they had been raising the destroyer, the value of scrap had gone down from £5 to less than £2 a ton.

But this did not make the slightest difference to Ernest Cox's plans. He had already decided to make the hull of the V.70 watertight, then pump her dry and use her as a floating workshop, and preparations for lifting the remainder of his scuttled ships went on as if nothing had happened to cloud the horizon. The remarkable thing was that salvage operations of this kind, and on this scale, constituted a completely new venture for both Ernest Cox himself and his technical staff, yet the remaining 24 destroyers were refloated within the next 20 months and, except for one setback, with an ease and regularity which bore no real relationship to the magnitude of the task involved.

When lifting operations for that year ceased in October, five more 750-ton destroyers had been refloated. In the following year, 1925, and working from March to December, 14 were raised in the 39 weeks, one of them in only four days. All this was achieved without working on Sundays, a rule which was never broken. Two of those raised in 1925 were larger vessels of 1,300 tons.

Some of the destroyers had been moored two or three abreast when they were scuttled and had gone to the bottom in a heap. There they presented a tangled up mass of anchors, cables, masts, funnels and guns which had to be untangled before any start could be made on preparations for actually lifting. In the course of years they became so much a part of the under-water scene that conger eels had taken up permanent residence in some of the more attractive holes which these wrecks provided for them free of charge. These vicious fish, and the occasional seal, gave the divers many a fright, as did 40-foot whales when making the ships' graveyard their playground.

By the middle of 1925, ten of the refloated destroyers had been made sufficiently seaworthy to be towed to Rosyth for breaking up, and half of Cox's outlay had been recovered.

Meanwhile a second and larger floating dock had been bought and towed to Lyness. It was a giant compared even with the original submarine-testing dock and its side walls were 40 feet high. The idea was to raise the big destroyers with the two L-docks, as with the smaller vessels, but then to manœuvre each one, after lifting, into the new large U-shaped dock which would be anchored nearby and already sunk on to the sea bed in readiness. After depositing the destroyer on the big dock's floor the two L-docks would be towed clear and the dock and destroyer raised in the usual way.

This was actually attempted with the first big destroyer, the G.103, but the two L-docks with the cradled destroyer slung beneath them were too much for the tugs to manœuvre into the gap between the walls of the big dock and this revolutionary idea was abandoned—but not altogether. The big dock was towed back to the beach where it underwent the same operation as its predecessor. One side wall was amputated, and the two L-docks then had a big brother, which was towed out to the scene of operations.

The G.103 was raised a second time and deposited sideways on to the floor of the big L-dock, then secured to the wall of the dock like an ordinary ship moored alongside a quay, but it was not a great success. The whole thing keeled over at an alarming angle and then the destroyer slid down the sloping floor, listing the dock so acutely that one corner of the floor struck the sea bed. The bottom tanks flooded and dock and destroyer sank gently to the bottom. Both were eventually refloated, but the accident resulted in one of the most difficult of all the Scapa Flow salvage operations—that of raising the damaged dock itself and its twice wrecked destroyer.

The remaining destroyers, including five more of 1,300 tons each which were refloated between February and April 1926, were all raised by the original method of lifting with the two L-dock sections.

Long before these smaller vessels were completely cleared from Gutter Sound, plans for raising the largest ship of the whole fleet, the great battle cruiser *Hindenburg*, were well advanced. On April 30th, 1926 the last destroyer to be tackled, the G.104, was successfully refloated; there was nothing, then, between Cox and the *Hindenburg*, but before preparations could be completed, something did intervene. The general strike of that summer caused the price of coal—life-blood of Cox's boilers and therefore of his pumps, generators and compressors—to soar so high that this vital fuel was, financially, almost beyond his means. But he was not to be so easily beaten. A check of the divers' surveys showed him that he had a coal mine of his own, and not only a coal mine but one full of ready dug coal. The mine was another battle cruiser, the *Seydlitz*. Lying on her side in only 65 feet of water, her high side was actually showing above the surface and inside the exposed armour plating were her coal bunkers, and full ones at that.

Admiral Ludwig von Reuter, on that summer day in 1919 when he saw the great *Hindenburg* sinking to the bottom in fulfilment of his cunning design, little thought that it would be his own coal which would help to raise her again, but so it was. The coal which Cox was able to scoop out of the *Seydlitz* kept his boilers going all through the general strike.

Even at high tide the *Hindenburg*'s great tripod mast, twin funnels and much of her upperworks remained uncovered. Like the V.70 and some of the other ships she was perfectly upright, and although she was in about 70 feet of water this was not nearly deep enough for her great bulk to be completely submerged. The big hull, 700 feet long on the waterline, 96 feet beam and displacing 28,000 tons, was too formidable a proposition to be refloated by the same methods that had proved so successful with the smaller ships.

Ernest Cox had already bought another ex-German floating dock from the Admiralty. He had cut it up, as before, and fitted out the two sections with workshops, generators, compressors, pumps and equipment for diving, kitchens and mess rooms. His plan was to use all four L-dock sections, two on either side of the *Hindenburg*, plug up all the holes in her hull and raise her by forcing air in and the water, thereby, out. She could then be towed to Rosyth for breaking up like any other old ship.

Hindenburg's holes were not damage holes but her own built-in ones—side and bottom valve openings, portholes, ventilators, hatchways and so on. A detailed survey by divers had confirmed that all the sea water valves were wide open and mostly damaged enough to prevent them being closed again, as was expected from the circumstances of her sinking.

The four dock sections were towed out to where the *Hindenburg* lay, half a mile west of the island of Cava, and moored in position, two on either side, by 16 anchors, four to each dock section. Some of these anchors weighed as much as nine tons each. Then two of the refloated destroyers were moored, one ahead and one astern of the *Hindenburg*, to act as breakwaters. Platforms were rigged between the docks and across to the *Hindenburg* so that the men could move about from one to the other easily and quickly.

The damaged bottom valves were sealed from the inside with quick-setting cement, but all other openings had to be plugged or patched and made watertight. The ship was, of course, completely flooded and so all this work had to be done by divers. The patches ranged in size from quite small ones covering portholes to one gigantic one 40 feet long and 21 feet wide, 6 inches thick and reinforced with 6-inch H-section steel girder. Weighing 11 tons when completed, it had been constructed ashore, then towed out, lifted by a crane on one of the docks and then lowered into position over the hole where one of the funnels had been. The other funnel was still watertight but the first one had become so badly corroded that it was found necessary to remove it entirely and patch the opening. It was a stupendous task, and just as well that not all of the patches had to be of this enormous size for there were, in all, just over 800 holes for which patches had to be made, bolted on and rendered watertight before pumping operations could even be thought about.

On August 5th all was ready. Eighteen pumps were connected to the various compartments in the hull and tested. Next day the pumping operations started in earnest but it was soon apparent that many of the patches were no longer watertight. Divers went down to investigate and found that the culprits were—fish. They were saithe, or coal-fish as they are more correctly called, a member of the cod family, and they had been busy eating, not the patches but the tallow which had been extensively used with the packing which made the patches watertight. The main problem then was how to make the tallow-eaters change their nasty habits. After some experimenting, the salvage officers found not only that cement and tallow mixed well and set firm underwater but that the saithe disliked the new mixture intensely.

It took the divers until the end of August to repack the leaking patches and then, when pumping was resumed, the old *Hindenburg* decided that she had sat on her bottom long enough, and tried to turn over. Whichever end they lifted first, a list developed, and when this reached the alarming angle of nearly 38 degrees it was obviously time to give way to her cantankerous behaviour and they lowered her to the bottom again while they pondered on a cure. But the *Hindenburg* seemed determined to spend at least one more winter in Scapa Flow. On September 2nd, and before anything could be started, a fierce north-westerly gale smashed so many of the patches that any further attempts to refloat her that year had to be abandoned.

South-east of the *Hindenburg*, between the islands of Cava and Rysa Little, lay the 23,000-ton battle cruiser *Moltke*, 610 feet long and over 96 feet beam. She had turned almost completely over when she sank and was now lying bottom up with a 17 degree list and in 78 feet of water. Her bottom valves and other hull openings could be sealed from the outside. She could then be made buoyant by expelling the water from inside her hull with compressed air, and her deck openings would provide ready-made vents for the expanding air as she rose to the surface. Ernest Cox had already decided that the *Moltke* was not only an ideal subject for this method, but that it was one which could be proceeded with at almost any time. So the docks were moved down to the *Moltke*.

That, at any rate, was the plan when divers started clearing the shoulder high tangle of weed from the *Moltke*'s bottom, using both knives and axes, for some of it had stems as thick as their own wrists.

As soon as the jungle of growth had been removed, the divers started on the job of plugging or otherwise sealing all the openings, and at last the sides and bottom were pronounced watertight once more. The compressors worked day and night, and at the end of ten days the fore end of the great battle cruiser broke surface. They stopped the forward compressors and concentrated on the after part, but after another 24 hours the stern was still down although the bow had risen still more. It was then clear that the main compartments were not airtight and that all the air being pumped in was rushing to the highest point. When it began bursting out from under the bow like a great submarine hurricane they decided it was time to stop pumping and let her settle down again on the bottom.

It was now the end of November, but they set to work at once on preparations for getting inside the hull to seal the transverse bulkheads and so divide the ship into airtight compartments. Although part of the *Moltke*'s bottom was just awash at low water, this operation entailed the construction and fitting of air locks and then cutting through the ship's bottom from inside the base of each airlock, so that the men could have access to the interior.

As soon as all the airlocks were fitted, divers went in to seal the leaks, working upwards towards the surface. The mess inside the *Moltke* was indescribable. Machinery and other things in a ship which are securely bolted down, and stay down under normal conditions, do not necessarily remain so when their world is suddenly turned upside down. On the inside of the deck of the upturned ship there was a sea of black mud which now enveloped everything which had fallen from its fastenings when she turned over and sank. Over all this débris the fuel oil had poured down through the tank air vents and broken pipes. For the latter part of the work they managed to maintain about ten feet of air space over the water level, but as this level began falling under the air pressure the floating oil was deposited over everything.

Notwithstanding these appalling working conditions, the hundreds of openings were eventually sealed and the hull effectively divided into three airtight sections—bow, stern and amidships. This work took them right through the winter and it was the end of March 1927, before they were ready for a second attempt. Bow and stern were raised independently with great success but as soon as they were lifted together the *Moltke*'s list increased alarmingly to over 33 degrees. Once more she was lowered to the bottom—and once more plans had to be revised.

The problem now was to prevent the starboard side from lifting. Twenty heavy lifting wires were passed from the dock, down underneath the wreck on the low, port side, and secured to the starboard side of the gun turrets. In addition, a destroyer hull and a pontoon were sunk and secured to the high, starboard side, to keep it down. The next attempt to raise the *Moltke* was a combined effort of tide, mechanical lift and compressed air and at first it appeared to be successful. She was listing, but much less than before. Then, with a noise like an explosion, one of the lifting wires parted, then another, followed by a third, and complete disaster was averted only by stopping the whole operation and slacking off the remaining wires. Air was released and she sank slowly back on to the bottom—for the third time that year.

When divers went down to investigate they found that the wires had been cut through at the sharp angle between deck and side. Metal pads were fitted over all the sharp edges in the way of the lifting wires and when new wire ropes had been fitted and secured to the gun turrets as before, they tried again. This time it was completely successful. When the bow broke water the list was just over 16 degrees but this decreased as the winches took the strain, and before the stern lifted it was less than 3 degrees. As the stern came up, the surrounding water suddenly exploded into waterspouts which shot 20 feet above the now visible bottom of the *Moltke*, showering everyone and everything with a mixture of water, oil and wet coal dust, and turning the sea into a cauldron. But it heralded no further disaster. The air inside the hull, which had been pressurized to almost 25 pounds per square inch in order to raise the stern off the sea bed, had rapidly expanded to the 9 or 10 pounds necessary to keep the bottom of the upturned hull about 20 feet out of the water—and all was well.

When the sea subsided and calm prevailed once more, it was seen with relief that the whole of the bottom of the great 23,000-ton battle cruiser was well clear of the water, on an even keel fore and aft, and with a list of only 2 degrees. Their first upside down refloating by compressed air had been achieved.

On June 16th, while being towed—still slung between the two docks—to Lyness pier on the first stage of her journey to Rosyth, the *Moltke* demonstrated her objection to such an undignified end by, almost literally, digging her heels in. She suddenly stopped, breaking one of the tow lines. The tugs pulled in all directions but nothing would move her and so divers went down to investigate. They found that one of the huge forward guns had dropped down to what would have been its greatest normal elevation, thereby thrusting its muzzle deep into the sea bed.

This mishap occurred at high water, so that the 11-inch gun barrel was pushed farther and farther into the bottom as the tide fell. A team of divers eventually blasted the offending gun free of the *Moltke*. A new set of lifting wires was then passed underneath the hull, and tightened up at low water. Then, with the help of the tide and compressed air, the *Moltke*—now seven feet higher than before—was successfully beached near Lyness pier.

The *Moltke*'s bottom, high and dry at all states of the tide, was then converted into a railway siding. The pier railway was taken up and relaid on piles right on to the upturned hull. The once proud battle cruiser of the German Navy then suffered the supreme indignity of having about 3,000 tons of her machinery and armour plate cut up and taken out through six foot square holes which had been cut in her bottom.

The great tow to Rosyth started on Friday, May 8th, 1928. The journey was a nightmare and she almost did not get there. Although the weather forecast was good when the tugs and their strange tow left Lyness, a sudden and unheralded easterly gale in the Pentland Firth nearly brought disaster to that most unusual of convoys, three ocean tugs with a 610-foot long battle cruiser floating bottom up. With seas breaking right over the wallowing hull, the deckhouses which had been built on the *Moltke*'s bottom—to provide shelter for the crew as well as protection for the compressors—were continually flooded. It was a frightening and nerve-racking day. The *Moltke* rolled to over 13 degrees and so much air escaped from inside the hull that she lost six feet of freeboard.

By nightfall they were in the calmer waters of the Moray Firth where one of the tugs was able to get alongside and restore the lost buoyancy by using her own compressors to augment those on the *Moltke*. But the salvaged battle cruiser was to survive yet another crisis before reaching her destination.

Approaching the Forth Bridge, the tugs found themselves heading for one channel while the *Moltke* seemed determined to pass under the adjoining span of the bridge. Tugs and tow could not, obviously, go their separate ways without a major accident. Seeing that the *Moltke* would probably pass through without touching the bridge piers, if she went by herself, the tugs hastily cast off their tow lines. The German battle cruiser, as if bent on one last glorious achievement before she ended her life at the shipbreakers, made a place for herself in the annals of maritime history by passing bottom up, engineless and all on her own, under the Forth Bridge. Above the bridge, the tugs took her in tow again and delivered her safely at Rosyth.

During the next three years Cox succeeded in raising six more capital ships. The third and successful attempt to refloat the *Hindenburg* did not take place until 1930. Before then, the battle cruiser *Seydlitz*, 656 feet long and displacing 25,000 tons, the battleship *Kaiser*, 24,500 tons, and a light cruiser, the *Bremse*, 4,200 tons, were all raised.

The *Seydlitz* was lying on her beam ends with her port side, like an island of steel, rising 20 feet above the water. Preparations for refloating her had started before the *Moltke* was raised, and work on the *Seydlitz* was well under way when the *Moltke* was beached at Lyness. Cox first attempted to raise the *Seydlitz* with compressed air, and with the ship lying, as she was, on her starboard side. Over 1,800 tons of armour plating, which was 12 inches thick amidships, was removed from her side above water in order to lower the centre of gravity, and then the sealing of bulkheads and openings went on throughout the latter half of 1927.

The patches required for some of the apertures, such as funnels and engine room ventilators, were even larger than those made for the *Moltke*. Patches for the funnel openings which had to be sealed from the inside, measured 46 feet by 29 feet and were made up from 12-inch timbers reinforced by steel girders, while patches for the larger ventilators covered an area of 450 square feet.

By June 1928, the hull had been converted into eight airtight sections, each capable of being pressurized individually. The water level inside was pressed down to about 21 feet below the level of the sea outside, and both bow and stern had been test-raised successfully. Then the bow and stern sections were pressurized together and the whole ship lifted off the bottom and everything appeared to be going well. Then a deep thud, like a muffled explosion, coming from somewhere deep down inside the hull, warned everyone of the disaster to come. Then another muffled bang as a second bulkhead gave way and the *Seydlitz*, like some huge hippopotamus which had been lying on its side in the water and was about to stand up, heaved her bow end right out of the water. This movement was accompanied by more explosive bangs and sounds of tearing steel. She turned another quarter of the way over; then her bottom came up and she sank beneath the water and settled on the sea bed, bottom uppermost, but at an angle of about 48 degrees. (Plate 7a.)

Divers found that the bridge and what was left of the mast, funnels and other superstructure were crushed against the sea bed and had prevented her from turning completely upside down. Cox, never accepted defeat, started all over again.

Now that she had become another *Moltke*, although with a far greater list, most of the patches would have to withstand much greater pressure, so that even the few remaining un-damaged ones had to be either renewed or made stronger. Cox now planned to refloat her upside down like the *Moltke*, and during the next four months all the upperworks, now 70 feet down, were cut away so that she could turn right over to the bottom-up position as soon as she was raised clear of the sea bed. New and taller airlocks were fitted to the curve of the hull between side and bottom, and all internal compartments made airtight again.

By early October they were ready for a second attempt but try as they might to turn her completely upside down by pressurizing the low side, she remained obstinate. At first she started coming back on to her side so they released the pressure and let her go down again. For the rest of the month they tried all sorts of devices and test-raised her bow or stern at least 40 times, but failed to reduce the list below 30 degrees.

In the end, Cox partially solved the problem by propping her up. He achieved this by raising her sufficiently for the divers to place some open-ended boilers upright on the sea bed underneath her low side. The boilers were then filled with quick-setting cement and the *Seydlitz* was gently lowered on to them, thus tilting her over to the required upside down position. When raised again with carefully controlled pressurization she listed to 25 degrees but became stable at that angle. Cox then resorted to a mechanically assisted lift as with the *Moltke*. The big L-shaped floating dock section was towed into position and pinned down to the low side of the *Seydlitz* with 24 heavy steel-wire ropes.

During the refloating operation on November 1st, half of the wires gave way under the strain but the remainder held and when she settled down after breaking surface with the usual turmoil, she did so with a list of only 8 degrees.

Like the *Moltke* she was beached alongside Lyness pier and had a railway laid on her bottom. Her heavy machinery was cut up and lifted out and her forward gun turret blasted off to reduce her draught. In May 1929 she was towed to Rosyth but her passage, too, was a frightening experience for everyone taking part.

Once again the fine weather forecast before the tugs set off with their tow from Lyness broke suddenly and unexpectedly. On the worst of the seven days passage they made only 17 miles in the 24 hours, and for over 14 of those—fortunately during the day—heavy seas swept the *Seydlitz* from end to end. The maintenance crew housed on the upturned hull had most of their equipment washed away but miraculously escaped with their lives.

The 24,500-ton battleship *Kaiser* had also turned over when she sank and was now lying bottom up with a list of only 8 degrees in 80 feet of water. Work on her had started in December 1928, long before the *Seydlitz* was raised. As a precaution against her behaving like the *Moltke* and the *Seydlitz*, and turning the wrong way when she left the bottom, Cox's divers built two 30-ton concrete pillars between the sea bed and the lower edge of the armour plating on the low side—but as it turned out, they were not needed after all.

Construction of air locks, patching and sealing went ahead without a hitch, and from the moment when the pressurized air began lifting her from the bottom, to her beaching on the island of Cava at the end of March 1929, she was completely under control.

Six weeks after the *Seydlitz* survived her rough seven day passage, the *Kaiser* followed her to Rosyth. She was the third of Cox's refloated ships to make the journey and, in complete contrast to the others, she had a fine and uneventful voyage.

Before they tackled the *Hindenburg* again, one more bottom-up refloating was achieved. When the light cruiser *Bremse*, of 4,200 tons, was scuttled in 1919 the British Naval party boarded her before she sank and tried to beach her on the bank off the southern point of Cava Island. As her bow touched bottom, she turned over and went down and was now lying almost upside down with her bow above the surface and her stern in 75 feet of water.

After blasting away her bridge and other superstructures, fitting airlocks, sealing and patching, wire ropes were passed underneath her low side from one of the docks moored alongside. Again the combined lifting effects of compressed air and mechanical power succeeded in bringing her to the surface in a completely upside down position, and she was refloated and towed to Lyness pier on the last day of November 1929.

Early in the following year Cox and his team, with a wealth of practical experience to draw on, now turned to the *Hindenburg* again and set to work with the ease and confidence which their expert knowledge now made possible. By the end of April 1930, divers had re-surveyed the hull and found to their relief that about 500 of the original 800 patches were still good, and so they began with the task of remaking or repairing the 300 which needed attention.

To improve her stability when she was refloated, the great forward gun turret, the tripod mast and most of the heavy superstructure were removed. Then, two enormous concrete pyramids 35 feet by 25 feet at the base tapering to 25 feet by 15 feet at the top, were built aft, one each side underneath her stern, to prevent her going over either way when her bow was raised.

The weather in the Orkneys was kind during that spring of 1930, and by the end of June everything was ready. On July 22nd she was successfully raised with only a slight list which was never more than 7 degrees. The great *Hindenburg*, after spending more than a decade on the bottom of Scapa Flow, was afloat again. Next day she was beached in Mill Bay. A month later, on August 23rd and in tow by three tugs, she set off on her last voyage. No gales blew up to hamper her passage to Rosyth and this final journey of hers was completed without incident on August 26th.

Another battle cruiser, the *Von der Tann*, 8,000 tons smaller than the *Hindenburg*, was refloated in the July of 1931, and after her it was the turn of the *Prinzregent Luitpold*, a sister ship of the *Kaiser*. The *Von der Tann* was bottom up and not far from where the *Hindenburg* had foundered west of Cava, where all the capital ships had been moored, but in deeper water—about 90 feet, and with a 17 degree list. This meant that the air locks on the low side had to be more than 40 feet high.

When the men got inside after the water had been pressed down, they found that the air was extremely foul, and although it was changed completely at least twice, explosive gases continued to rise from what must have been a considerable quantity of decaying matter in some part of the hull. On one occasion when the work of sealing the bulkheads was well under way, three of the men with water up to their knees were cutting through a pipe with an oxyacetylene torch. Gas was coming through the pipe from the section on the other side of the bulkhead, and this became ignited by the torch and then exploded. Thomas McKenzie, one of the two joint chief salvage officers, who was standing at the bottom of a ladder ten feet from the open door of the cabin in which the men were working, shot upwards, struck his head on the hatch coaming above and fell back, unconscious, into the knee-deep water.

The explosion, which had actually occurred on the other side of the bulkhead, blew the shattered plating across the cabin, injuring two of the men and blocking the doorway. The pressure of the air in the cabin, now open to the after section because of the shattered bulkhead, was suddenly released and the water rose rapidly until it was up to the chins of the three trapped men. All the lights had been put out by the explosion, and the men—now in utter darkness—could only hope that help would reach them before anything happened to allow the water to rise even higher.

They were saved by a rescue party who cut through the two-inch armour plated deck above them to bring them out. The unconscious McKenzie, in danger of being drowned, was also discovered in time, but his severe head injury put him on the sick list for over two months.

Such were the dangers which Cox's men risked and endured, without serious loss of enthusiasm, throughout their seven years of operations on the scuttled German fleet. The *Von der Tann* was refloated towards the end of November and then beached on Cava. After that, everyone enjoyed a long and most welcome Christmas break, and the *Von der Tann* was not moved to Lyness until February.

With the great economic slump of the 1930s already begun and the price of scrap metal falling disastrously, Cox decided to leave the refloated battle cruiser where she was and raise the *Prinzregent Luitpold* which, although a sister to the *Kaiser* turned out to be another *Von der Tann*. Like the *Von der Tann* she was almost bottom up, and had a similar list, but she had sunk in nearly 110 feet of water which meant the erection of airlocks over 60 feet high. Again like the *Von der Tann*, the air became foul inside as soon as it was pumped in, and on May 27th an explosion caused an accident which was much worse than any before. It resulted in the death of one of the men and severe burns to three others.

The tragic accident and loss of life caused only a temporary hindrance. The *Prinzregent Luitpold* was refloated on an even keel and with her bottom 10 feet out of the water on July 6th. Ten days later she joined the *Von der Tann* at Lyness.

Although Cox was the owner of one more battleship on the bottom at Scapa Flow, the 28,000-ton *Bayern*, he decided to leave her where she was, and pack up and go home. He disposed of the *Bayern* and all his plant to a Scottish shipbreaking company, which afterwards became absorbed by the Metal Industries Group. By the time his working party had cleared up at Lyness it was 1933 and the price of scrap metal had started to rise again. Both the *Von der Tann* and the *Prinzregent Luitpold* were towed to Rosyth in the late spring of that year and sold for a reasonable price to the breakers. (Plate 8*a*.)

Metal Industries decided to continue clearing the sunken remnants of the German wartime Naval Fleet from Scapa Flow. Including the *Bayern* there were still six large capital ships to be dealt with, all of them bottom up and in deeper water than any already raised—between 120 and 155 feet.

Although Cox had said goodbye to Scapa Flow to develop his already flourishing scrap metal business, Thomas McKenzie did not sever his connection with the salvage operations and it was he who supervised the refloating of the *Bayern* in 1933. The battleship was lying on a sloping sea bed with 65 feet of water over her hull at the bow, and 85 feet over her stern. The seven airlocks which had to be fitted to the bottom to give access to the hull interior were enormous tapering cylinders, seven feet across at the base and ranging from 70 feet to 90 feet in height. The tallest weighed 20 tons, and the fitting of the airlocks to the bottom of the ship in such deep water was no easy task for the divers.

On July 8th, following the bursting of a main drainage pipe in one of the sections, compressed air rushed into the forward part and caused a premature refloating of the bow which rose nearly 10 feet out of the water. Then the stern came up and the whole ship was afloat, but listed heavily to starboard before steadying up at about 29 degrees, and so the stern was decompressed and allowed to sink to the bottom again. Divers found that the *Bayern* had shed all four gun turrets, weighing about 2,500 tons, and left them on the bottom. The resultant raising of the centre of gravity caused a lot of extra work before she was finally refloated.

At the initial attempt to raise her some weeks later she first turned completely bottom up and then rolled the other way so much that she seemed about to go right over on her side. When the list reached 42 degrees, air was quickly released from the sections on the high side and she sank back on to the bottom with a heavy list to port. The shorter airlocks were now on the low side and completely under water, and the mishap necessitated extending some of the airlocks to 100 feet or more before work inside the hull could be completed. When the *Bayern* was eventually raised, on September 1st, she came up on an even keel and floated with the bottom 10 feet out of the water. She made a fantastic picture with each of the seven airlocks looking rather like an elongated Leaning Tower of Pisa, built on an island of barnacles. Next day she made her four mile journey in tow to shallow water near Lyness. (Plate 7*b*.)

Between 1933 and 1938, four more battleships, the *König Albert*, *Kaiserin*, *Grosser Kurfurst* and the *Friedrich der Grosse* were raised and disposed of. The fifth and last before the outbreak of the Second World War brought the salvage operations to a halt, was the 26,600-ton *Derflinger*, 710 feet long and 99 feet beam. She, too, had turned over when she sank and was now resting on the sea bed, north-west of the island of Cava, at a greater depth than any of the others. With a list of over 20 degrees, at high tide there was 90 feet of water over her bilge on one side and 110 feet over the other which necessitated airlocks of a size which dwarfed even the lengthened ones on the *Bayern*. The tallest of the airlocks used on the *Derflinger* were 130 feet high and weighed 30 tons. All of these airlocks were constructed ashore and made up from 10 foot sections of tubular steel. As each one was completed it was slung from the jib of a floating crane and carried out to the *Derflinger*.

Nine airlocks were used and the hull was divided into seven airtight sections. The work of sealing and patching her occupied the salvage team for eight months and the refloating of the *Derflinger* proved to be a smooth but spectacular operation— and a fitting reward for the months of strenuous and dangerous effort. Men working inside the hull had been subjected to a pressure of over 64 lb. to the square inch because of the great depth, and had required one and a half hours decompression after each of their one hour daily shifts.

In the twenty years the *Derflinger* had been on the bottom, her superstructure had sunk deep into the mud and because of this and the depth involved, nearly 160 feet, enormous pressure was required to provide enough buoyancy to break the bottom suction. To reduce this to a minimum, the refloating was timed to take place at low water.

As she slowly freed herself from her bed of mud the upward movement was shown by the airlocks gradually rising out of the water. At first the rate of lift was only about two feet a minute. Then, in a matter of seconds, she broke surface in a turmoil of air, water, mud and oil which had shot out of the lower apertures (left open for the purpose) as the pressure outside decreased and now exploded around the heaving hull and rose 150 feet into the air.

When everything had quietened down, divers went below to see if she, too, had left her gun turrets on the bottom. All was well with the turrets but there were certain parts of the superstructure low enough to cause trouble on the way in, and these were cut away. Next day the *Derflinger* was towed inshore at high tide and grounded in only 60 feet of water, where she remained moored with eight heavy anchors while further work inside was carried out so that she could be raised to the level required for moving her to Rosyth, but here the Second World War intervened. The dry dock at Rosyth was required by the Admiralty for other and more important ships, and the *Derflinger* was towed into Rysa Sound, moored with 10 anchors and left there for the next seven years.

Her end came in 1946 when she made her last passage on tow

to the Clyde. There, moored off Rosneath, was a giant 30,000-ton floating dock which Metal Industries had just bought from the Admiralty, and into the dock went the *Derflinger* upside down. While the dock was kept submerged just below the *Derflinger*'s superstructure, divers worked for four weeks building blocks on the floor of the dock so that the weight of the ship would be evenly distributed. When every aperture was sealed she was undocked and towed into Gareloch to the shipbreakers' wharf at Faslane. Fifteen months later she had gone the way of her predecessors and was completely demolished.

The wheel had turned full circle. The nation which had made her Navy thirty years before to do battle in the First World War had since built another Navy and brought about a Second World War. That second Navy, too, was now vanquished and if the *Derflinger* had been given a memory one wonders what her thoughts would have been as the shipbreakers reduced her mutilated and rusting hull to just so many thousand tons of scrap metal.

CHAPTER EIGHT

THE *EGYPT*

On the evening of May 20th, 1922 the French cargo ship *Seine*, bound from La Pallice on the west coast of France to Le Havre, was approaching Ushant where the Bay of Biscay meets the English Channel. In good, clear weather she would have been about to converge with other ships making for Ushant from across the Bay, and preparing to meet outward-bound ships which had already rounded Ushant and were on course for Finisterre.

But the weather on that May evening was not good. What would otherwise have been a fine calm night to come was marred by a cold dense fog. Wary of the rock-fringed island of Ushant and its treacherous approaches, the *Seine* headed north-westward so as to be sure of rounding it at a safe distance. Ushant was no place to go looking for in that weather.

About the same time, the P. & O. liner *Egypt*, having already cleared Ushant, was on course for Finisterre. She had left Tilbury the previous day with 291 crew and 44 passengers to call at Marseilles, where the majority of her usual passengers for India would be joining, en route for Bombay. Those other passengers, could they have known, were missing far more than a possibly rough crossing of the Bay of Biscay.

It was just about 7 p.m. and still bright daylight up above, but on the smooth unruffled sea there was dark dank fog. One could see barely 30 yards and both ships were proceeding cautiously, sounding their sirens. Then the *Egypt* heard another ship's fog signal on her port bow, and presumably the other vessel heard the *Egypt*'s siren, for both continued blowing, the one answering the other. But fog plays fearful tricks, with both volume and direction of sound, and suddenly the bow of a ship loomed up out of the swirling murk and struck the *Egypt* on her port side, between her two funnels.

It was a deadly blow. She was severely gashed below the water line and immediately began to settle by the stern with a list to port. The *Seine*, after drawing clear, lost the *Egypt* in the fog but soon found her again and started picking up survivors. The *Egypt*'s radio operator had time to send out her estimated position, which was given as 48 degrees 10 minutes North, 5 degrees 30 minutes West, and continued to transmit S-O-S until the ship went down, taking him with her.

Land's End Radio picked up her distress signal at 7.2 p.m. and French radio stations also heard her call. Two of the French stations, Ushant and Pointe du Raz, took directional bearings of the signals but as the *Seine* was on the spot, and picking up survivors, no great importance was attached to the precise position indicated by the intersection of the two bearings.

The *Egypt* sank within 20 minutes of the collision, but the *Seine* stayed in the area for nearly three hours searching for further survivors. Of the 335 passengers and crew on board, a total of 96 went down with the *Egypt* or were lost in the fog and drowned. The 239 who were saved were landed at Brest early the following morning.

That same morning some mail bags and floating wreckage from the *Egypt* were picked up by a British destroyer four miles north of the position given by the *Egypt* the night before. Nothing else was found.

The 8,000-ton ship had gone down in over 400 feet of water and taken with her not only people, whom neither gold nor silver could ever replace, but gold and silver itself. Consigned by the Bank of England to Indian banks, the *Egypt* had been carrying 1,089 gold bars, 1,199 ingots of silver and 164,979 sovereigns—over 45 tons in all and worth, at that time, £1,083,528. It is, perhaps, interesting to reflect that in 1970

96

that amount of bullion and specie would be valued at more than four times that sum.

The strong room which held this most valuable consignment of cargo was five decks down and across the middle of the ship, and with the wreck itself in over 400 feet of water the problems of finding it and then recovering the bullion presented such enormous difficulties that salvage, at that time, was considered impracticable. In 1922, no recovery operation which first entailed blasting open a wreck at such a depth had ever been successfully undertaken. In the history of marine salvage, no such difficulties had ever been overcome and Lloyd's London underwriters, who covered most of the £1,170,152 insurance, accepted the loss—the heaviest in the annals of the Institution—and settled the claims within seven days.

Although the *Egypt* and her treasure were thought to be lost for ever, the wreck was destined not to be left in peace. The first attempt to locate the *Egypt* with a view to possible salvage of the bullion was made in the spring of 1923 when the Salvage Association on behalf of the underwriters, entered into an agreement with two London consulting engineers, Peter Sandberg C.B.E. and James Swinburne, whereby 'Messrs. Sandberg and Swinburne, being of the opinion that it might be possible to salve part of the cargo of SS *Egypt*' undertook 'to endeavour to locate the wreck and to salve the specie and/or bullion and/or coin on board the vessel'.

Peter Sandberg and James Swinburne then engaged a Swedish firm, the Gothenburg Towage and Salvage Company, to make an attempt to find the *Egypt*. The company's salvage vessel *Fritjof* and two large steam trawlers began sweeping operations on May 22nd, 1923, and nearly a month later found a large obstruction very near to the position indicated by the radio bearings taken by Ushant and Pointe du Raz, details of which Peter Sandberg had obtained from the French Ministry of Marine. Captain Gustaf Hedback, in command of the *Fritjof*, seemed to have little doubt that what they had found was, in fact, the *Egypt*. They recorded the position as accurately as possible, ceased operations and returned to Sweden, intending to go back to the area the following year with deep diving equipment. But the Gothenburg Towing and Salvage Company decided otherwise; the search had already cost them £2,000 and they concluded that the very slender chances of successful salvage did not justify any further expense. So the project was abandoned.

Then, in June 1925, a French company took up the challenge, when Peter Sandberg and James Swinburne contracted with the Union d'Entreprises Sousmarines for another attempt to find the wreck and bring up the bullion. They were some time making up their minds exactly how to go about it and it was not until the following year that the search was started, but it did not last long. The French salvage company and their own sub-contractors, La Société Nouvelle des Pêcheries à Vapeur, using two vessels carrying German divers equipped with Neufeldt and Kuhnke articulated diving shells, swept the area throughout May and June of 1926. They gave up without locating the elusive wreck although it was disclosed afterwards that at one stage, when working very near to the position where the *Fritjof* claimed to have caught on something with her sweep, one of the divers thought he saw a dark mass resembling a wreck. But again, an alleged discovery which could have been the *Egypt* was not confirmed, and one wonders why. Perhaps it was just wishful thinking.

It was now more than four years since the ship and her treasure had gone to the bottom. Two unsuccessful attempts to find her had been made but still Peter Sandberg did not give up. He was convinced, perhaps beyond all ordinary reason at that time, that the *Egypt* could be found and sufficient gold recovered to justify all that the seemingly impossible task might entail. Two more years passed and still his faith in the idea had not died.

There was in Italy at that time a company by the name of Società Recuperi Marittimi, known as SORIMA; it had achieved great success in the use of deep-diving apparatus and had made some remarkable recoveries from considerable depths. In 1928 SORIMA was engaged to make yet another attempt to locate the wreck of the *Egypt* and recover the gold.

In June 1929, two small salvage vessels belonging to SORIMA commenced operations. They were the *Artiglio* and the *Rostro*, and were fitted out for laying moorings, deep diving, sweeping for wrecks and everything else which their search might entail, as well as for recovering the bullion should their mission meet with success. On board the *Artiglio* there were modified Neufeldt and Kuhnke articulated diving shells, SORIMA's own observation turrets and a varied assortment of grabs. They were well prepared for anything—and everything.

Early in June 1929, *Artiglio* and *Rostro* started sweeping for the *Egypt* around the position where Captain Hedback of the *Fritjof* thought he had found a large wreck in 1923. Commendatore Giovanni Quaglia, who had originally formed SORIMA, personally took charge of the operations.

After several days of getting their wire sweep caught up almost as soon as the two vessels started moving, he decided that the sea bed in the area was too rocky for sweeping with an unsupported wire rope. Although they were 15 miles to the westward of Ar Men buoy which was moored in over 200 feet of water and two miles to seaward of the western extremity of the Chaussée de Sein, this rocky spur seemingly continued deep down right into the search area. With the water between 250 and 400 feet deep it was safe enough there for shipping but a difficult and dangerous area in which to sweep for a wreck.

Perhaps it was one of the larger of these submerged rocks, and not the *Egypt* or any other wreck, which Captain Hedback had found in 1923 and perhaps it is more than just a mere coincidence that a few years later there appeared on the Admiralty charts of the area a sounding of '22 fathoms—Rock' in the position of Captain Hedback's 'wreck'. There was a rocky hill there, with only 132 feet of water over the top, in general surrounding depths of over 350 feet.

The *Artiglio* and the *Rostro*—tiny vessels by comparison with their mammoth task, for both were converted steam trawlers and the larger, the *Artiglio*, was only about 90 feet long—returned to Brest where Quaglia held a conference to review the whole situation. There were really three positions to be taken into consideration. The central one was that given by the *Egypt* herself after the collision. Four miles north of that was where the mail bags and wreckage had been found. Four miles south of the *Egypt*'s position was where Captain Hedback claimed to have found something. All three positions were on a line running north and south, but the *Egypt* had been on a course of 207 degrees from Ushant to Finisterre.

Quaglia therefore decided to establish a search area which embraced all three positions and covered an area of two and a half miles on either side of the *Egypt*'s track—40 square miles of sea bed, 400 feet deep, in which to search for a wrecked ship—an area 48,000 feet by 30,000 feet in which to hunt blindly for a ship 500 feet by 54 feet.

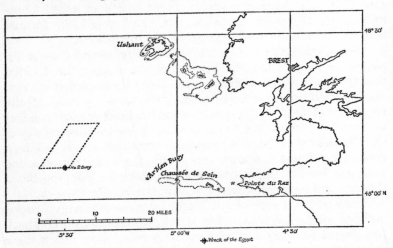

Next morning the *Rostro* went out to mark the limits of their parallelogram-shaped search area with seven buoys. Each mooring consisted of a 4-ton anchor, 50 feet of heavy chain cable, 400 feet of steel-wire rope and a 1-ton buoy, and she laid one mooring at each corner, one in the centre and one half-way along each of the two long sides. The *Artiglio* was to go out on the following day to start sweeping but by that time the wind was nearing gale force; the *Rostro* returned to Brest where both vessels were weather-bound for a whole week.

That week was not entirely wasted. Quaglia obtained details of all the radio messages and signals which had been received from the *Egypt* before she sank, and these shifted the weight of evidence to the southern part of the buoyed area. Ushant had recorded a radio bearing of 217 degrees and Pointe du Raz one of 277 degrees. These produced a position only two miles west of where Captain Hedback thought he had found a wreck and so Quaglia decided to try this area again.

In those days, before navigational aids and sonar devices such as Decca, radar and Asdic were available, the accurate plotting of positions out of sight of land was extremely difficult. The *Egypt* had sunk more than 20 miles from the nearest light-house and 25 miles from the nearest land. Radio bearings are subject to error, especially during twilight, and, as with positions obtained from visual bearings on lighthouses or other landmarks, where a bearing of one degree results in a position discrepancy of 100 feet for every mile of distance, the resultant plot is not always precise. This uncertainty of position, in an area where tidal streams of two and a half knots are experienced, did nothing to lighten their task.

On June 18th the two little ships resumed their search around Captain Hedback's position and along the southern boundary of the search area. They laid marker buoys to provide means of checking their position and the progress of their search, and used a wire rope sweep weighted with chain. Time after time the sweep caught on something and held fast, only to slip free before the object could be investigated by the diver—which could be done only at slack water. Once they snagged on some-thing when they were just over half a mile west of Captain Hedback's position, which was marked by No. 2 Buoy. The weather was far from perfect and a fresh north-easterly wind and rising sea were beginning to make conditions both uncom-fortable and difficult. They hove in on the wire sweep until both parts were leading straight down. They were bar tight and seemed as if they were sawing to and fro on something hard. The observation turret was put over but the tide was too strong and carried the diver right away until he was no more than 50 feet below the surface.

It was taken aboard again and they dropped a marker buoy in case the sweep wire carried away before the tide eased sufficiently for the diver to go down, but after hanging on for three hours in worsening weather, the wire snapped. When they hove it aboard they found that the frayed ends bore traces of rust and what looked suspiciously like white paint. The

Egypt's colours had been black and buff, but during the war she had been a hospital ship—and painted white. The white would still be underneath the black and the buff, but whether or not it was the *Egypt* they had found, they were never to know. Next day the weather was still too bad for diving and both ships returned to Brest. By the time they were able to resume operations the marker buoy had disappeared.

It could well have been that the spot they had marked was, in fact, the *Egypt*, for it was precisely there that they eventually found her.

In Brest, Quaglia had received a letter from one Father Innocent, a Capuchin friar and also a professional metal diviner, who offered to find the *Egypt* and her gold. Encouraged by reports of Father Innocent's successes in Italy, Quaglia agreed to let him try his powers at sea and he was taken out in the *Artiglio*. With the ship secured to No. 2 Buoy, Father Innocent claimed he could sense the presence of a steel ship and some gold about half a mile to the eastward. During the night the *Artiglio* changed places with the *Rostro* which was moored to another buoy some distance off, and next morning the good Father—knowing nothing of the overnight exchange of positions, again found his ship and her gold, still half a mile to the eastward. He was sent home forthwith.

Father Innocent's visit to Brest, and his association with the search for the *Egypt*, had attracted considerable publicity which was followed by a host of other offers to find the bullion, mostly for 10 per cent or so of the resultant prize. When the ships were again weather-bound in Brest—they were beset by bad weather right through that summer of 1929—a certain Monsieur Poireau turned up with a collection of gadgets and claimed that he could find the *Egypt* by taking bearings from the land. Here was a human mobile Direction Finding Station and, probably with more amusement than seriousness, Quaglia let him try. They were held up by the weather, anyway, and so had nothing to lose, but after two attempts to locate the *Egypt* had failed M. Poireau also took his leave. The day had been misty and he could not see much of the shore line, but they lost faith in his methods when he first 'found' the wreck in the direction of Spain and then produced bearings which put it well north of

Plate 9*a*, The *Raffio*

9*b*, Gianni, chief diver on first
Artiglio

9*c*, Mooring with sinker, for laying
by *Artiglio*

Plate 10*a*, The *Niagara*, entering Paget Sound, Vancouver

Plate 10*b*, Model of *Niagara*, showing explosions

Ushant. He, too, went home and Quaglia returned to more orthodox searching.

Still convinced by the weight of evidence that the *Egypt* was more likely to be found in the southern half of the area, Quaglia spent the rest of the summer—such as it was—systematically sweeping the 20 square miles south of the *Egypt*'s own estimated position. They found nothing except rock ledges and in the end, disappointed and somewhat discouraged, they gave up and suspended operations for the winter.

Bad weather had been their worst enemy, and their spells at sea had rarely lasted for more than two or three days. Their search area was, of course, wide open to the Atlantic. The nearest land to the westward was 2,000 miles away while, from the south-west, wind and weather had an uninterrupted run of 3,500 miles from the West Indies and the coast of Florida. But that first season had given them all valuable experience and knowledge. Frequent investigation of objects caught by the sweep had shown them that the sea bed was mostly hard flat sand with wedge-shaped rocky outcrops up to 15 feet high. They also knew that the observation turret could remain at depths of up to 400 feet for periods of up to two hours between tides and with no ill effects on the diver.

SORIMA had other work to do besides looking for the *Egypt*, and it was not until the following June that the search was resumed. Unfortunately, another would-be helper's advice resulted in their attention being diverted to the northern half of the area and another two wasted months. Captain Le Barzic, who had been in command of the *Seine* when she sank the *Egypt* in 1922, went to Brest and told Quaglia that he had checked his own position at the time, and was quite sure that he had been several miles to the north of where Captain Hedback said he had found a large wreck.

For more than eight weeks, in that summer of 1930, the *Artiglio* methodically swept the northern half of the buoyed area. At first she had the help of both the *Rostro* and a third vessel, a small converted Japanese trawler renamed *Raffio*, but later the *Rostro* was replaced by the *Raffio*. (Plate 9a.)

Small buoys were laid to mark each day's sweeping area and shifted gradually southward. By the beginning of August the northern half had been so thoroughly searched that Quaglia felt certain that the *Egypt* was not there. They had learned to discard rocks without going to the extent of a diver's investigation and had actually found some wrecks in the area, but these were small enough or old enough for the diver to discard them also without detailed examination.

August 1930, was drawing to a close. Although their search for the *Egypt* had started only the previous year and was not, therefore, being unusually prolonged, the nature of their objective had made it the subject of much comment. One of the many suggestions put forward by others who sought to explain just why the *Egypt* had not been found, was that she had probably drifted some miles after sinking and before she reached the bottom. This might have been possible in the deepest part of the Pacific Ocean; it was certainly not possible 25 miles south-west of Ushant, in spite of the strong tides, where the depth of water was almost 100 feet less than the length of the *Egypt* herself. It was afterwards established that the stern of the *Egypt* had, in fact, been grinding on the sea bed before the bow became completely submerged.

By August 27th they had already spent a week or so systematically sweeping nearer Captain Hedback's position, using lines of buoys to mark their progress and to avoid over-lapping. On that day, while working about a mile to the westward of the point and southward of their line of five marker buoys, their sweep held fast on something, but the freshening wind was making the sea too rough for diving. They marked the position with a buoy, recovered their sweep and went back into harbour for the night. The blow was short-lived and they were out again the following morning. When they reached the position they found that the marker buoy had survived the rough night and was still there, but the easternmost of the five sweeping buoys was missing. Then someone spotted it about half a mile away and the *Artiglio* steamed across to retrieve it before it drifted out of sight. Probably the sinker wire had carried away, they thought, but as soon as the buoy itself was recovered they knew by the weight on the wire that the sinker was still attached. Not only that, but the wire or the sinker had caught on to something as well. The weight was more than the sinker alone.

They heaved slowly and at first it seemed as though it was held fast by something below, then the 'something' gave way and the wire started coming in again, but it still seemed to be lifting more than its own sinker. It was, and although that 'something' was not gold, it could not have been of any greater value. The wire had twisted itself around a small davit. The davit could have come only from a wreck—and that wreck could be the *Egypt*. They dropped a marker buoy on the spot and studied the drawings of the ship they hoped was lying down there beneath them. The davit was much too small to be one of her boat's but she could have had a small davit for a gangway or something like that. Quaglia compared the size of the one they had just recovered with that of every davit on the drawings, and found one, right on the stern, which fitted exactly.

Was it stretching fantasy too far to suggest that the gremlins had taken compassion on them and guided their drifting buoy right on to the elusive *Egypt*? They would have to wait until the following day to know, for it was already too late for their hopes to be confirmed and their fears dispelled—or otherwise—before nightfall. The *Raffio* kept watch on the buoy marking their precious find and, at first light, started laying a circle of moorings around the position. As soon as the *Artiglio* was secured in the centre, right alongside the marker, the observation turret was put over. Inside the turret Bargellini, one of *Artiglio*'s three divers, adjusted his eyes to the underwater gloom and then spoke on his telephone to Gianni, the chief diver, nearly 400 feet above him. Yes, there was a wreck down there—and a large one. In slow cautious moves under Bargellini's directions, the *Artiglio* moved him nearer, then up a few feet and then along at deck level while he peered at the dim shape of the wreck and tried to pick out some details. (Plate 9*b*.)

Up above, the clouds which had been obscuring the sun were moving away. For a few minutes the sun shone brightly, and filtered down through the water, enabling Bargellini to describe briefly a hydraulic cargo crane which he could just see. On the *Artiglio*'s bridge, Quaglia and Gianni were scanning the *Egypt*'s drawings and comparing Bargellini's description with just such a crane. Almost certainly, they had found the *Egypt* at last.

By noon the following day a thorough survey of the wreck left them in no doubt. There she lay, almost upright on a hard sand bottom, 396 feet down, in an area of scattered rocks. There was a gash in her port side where the *Seine*'s bow had cut through her plates, and her stern was smashed and almost unrecognizable. The *Egypt*, with her gold and her silver—treasure worth more than £1,000,000—which had eluded her seekers for over eight years, was there beneath them. Their search was over. It was Saturday, August 30th, 1930.

The position of the wreck was later established as 48 degrees 6 minutes North, 5 degrees 30 minutes West, less than a mile west-north-west of the point of intersection of the two radio bearings of her S-O-S signals after the collision.

By Sunday evening, Gianni had found the place where they had already decided to commence blasting, but before they started on that task, Quaglia wanted to have some tangible proof with which to satisfy the sceptics ashore. Two days later, the *Artiglio* went into Brest with flags flying and with one of the *Egypt*'s hydraulic cranes on board. Five tons of the *Egypt* went into harbour in the hold of the little *Artiglio*—and everyone knew that the *Egypt* had been found.

Before blasting began in earnest, Quaglia made one more recovery. When the *Artiglio* went out again after landing the crane, and her sweeping gear—they had finished with that for good—he decided to break out the Captain's safe in the hope that he would find something of value in it, to add to the crane next time they went in. Under Bargellini's directions from the observation turret, the big grapnel was lowered and after some manœuvring they managed to get it under the 'roof' of the Captain's cabin. After a few heaves the top of the cabin came away and the diver could actually see the safe inside. Then they lowered the scissors grab, got hold of the safe and brought it up. Unfortunately it contained nothing but a sodden mass of papers, but as a sudden westerly gale forced them into Brest for shelter before anything else could be achieved, at least they had something more to show the critics.

By the end of September they had cleared away some deck-houses which were in the way and cut down through the boat deck. They were actually making a start on the upper deck when the early onset of winter gales forced a suspension of operations.

With their well-earned success behind them and every prospect that 1931 would see a break through to the strong room and recovery of at least some of the gold, the *Artiglio* and her crew went off to work on the wreck of an ammunition ship in more sheltered waters at the entrance to St. Nazaire, all unsuspecting of the cruel fate which awaited them. Their job was to cut away the upper part of the wreck so as to leave a depth of at least 40 feet over the top. On December the 7th, the charge which would have completed the operation exploded the whole of the ammunition in the sunken ship. The *Artiglio* was completely engulfed by the terrifying inrush of water into the 200-foot basin caused by the explosion, and all three divers as well as two other members of the crew and the *Artiglio* herself were lost.

It was a great tragedy for SORIMA, for the families of those who were never to see the fulfilment of the *Egypt* operations, and for those who were left.

SORIMA acquired an old Newfoundland Banks fish carrier and converted her into another and larger *Artiglio*. In the last week of May 1931 she left Brest to resume work on the *Egypt* but after relaying the moorings with 7-ton concrete sinkers in place of the 5-ton anchors, to suit her greater length of 150 feet, fog and bad weather prevented any diving until Friday June 5th, and even then it was Saturday before they found the *Egypt* again. She was nearby, but 'nearby' was not close enough, and the diver spotted her again only after hours of moving around. One wonders how many times they had been as close as that, and passed her by, during their months of searching.

But still they were bedevilled by bad weather and it was to be another whole week before they were able to resume blasting their way down to the bullion room. Mario, the new chief diver, after surveying the situation himself, proposed that they should cut the decks away right across from side to side, and for a distance of about 50 feet between the forward funnel and the bridge, and this they proceeded to do.

The explosive charges used by the *Artiglio* consisted of iron tubes eight feet long and four inches in diameter, packed with blasting gelignite and fired by means of an electric charge through an inserted detonator. To cut across the deck they used two of these eight foot tubes, lashed end to end on a wooden spar. Mancini, the second diver, went down in the observation turret to check his position and then the first bomb was lowered, but it was not until several hours later that it was finally placed in the desired position. There were hours of moving this way and that, a few feet at a time, of lowering the bomb and then raising it again for yet another move—then down again. If one thinks of a swaying crane, perched on top of a 400-foot high skeleton building, trying to land a 16-foot long pipe on to a marked position on the third floor, which the crane driver cannot see, under telephoned directions from a man he cannot see either, then the 'several hours' may be easily accounted for.

At last, when the bomb was in position, the lowering wire was slipped and the observation turret brought up. Only then, when the diver was well clear of the water, was the bomb fired. At least, the actions of firing it were carried out on deck, but nothing happened. The firing wire had broken near the bottom and there was nothing they could do about it. They were confronted with one of the most dangerous situations in submarine blasting, that of having an unexploded bomb in position on a wreck, with the detonating wire broken.

The usual way of getting rid of it is by placing another bomb alongside it, and then firing the second one in the hope that the first will be detonated by the explosion of the second. This was eventually achieved during the course of the afternoon. The explosion was like the crack of an anti-aircraft gun being fired immediately below them and the resultant shock waves made the *Artiglio* shudder as if stricken with ague.

Through the rest of June and all through July they blasted, grabbed the wreckage, dumped it clear and blasted again whenever the wind and tide allowed them to work, which it did not do for most of the time. June had given them no more than 11 days which were suitable for diving; July gave only half that number, and August was almost as bad. September was a little kinder, the equinoctial gales being far less fierce and less frequent than usual. It began to look as if the weather gods were relenting and had decided to allow them to retrieve at least some of the treasure before the year was out—by reversing the seasons for their special benefit. October was, in fact, better than July and then they continued to strive on through November, but their respite was soon over and they were beaten at last by winter and the fading light. Beaten—but only just.

Since resuming work in June, they had cut down through four decks and the *Egypt* was now almost in two pieces. They had actually cut a hole in the top of the bullion room large enough for the observation turret to enter, and on November 17th Mancini was able to look down into the room for the first time. Much to his surprise the dark cavern appeared to be almost full of cargo of some sort but, of course, after nearly 10 years under the water it was unlikely that boxes of gold would be recognizable as such in that murky submarine gloom.

Working periods were getting shorter and shorter and the light so bad that, in the end, the observation turret was bumping against a wreck which the diver could not even see. They managed to remove one more deck plate from above the bullion room and made several attempts to get the small specially designed grab down through the hole, but to no avail. The diver could see neither the wreck nor the grab.

With a rising southerly wind whipping the sea into breaking crests, they were forced to give up with nothing but a broken wreck to show for their three seasons' work. It was December 2nd 1931, when, for the third year in succession operations were suspended for the winter.

Before they resumed in the middle of the following May, Quaglia had to face a financial crisis. The salvage attempt had already cost him £80,000 and the first bar of gold had still to be recovered, but he managed to survive by securing sufficient working capital to embark on yet another year of endeavour. His reward was almost in sight, but much farther away than the few days he thought it would be when he set out from Brest on that bright spring morning in May.

Removal of the main deck in the way of the bullion room necessitated more blasting. The towering jagged edges of the severed decks on both sides were an awe-inspiring sight for the diver peering through the windows of his observation turret, as it sank slowly down into the yawning chasm which they had blasted out of the submerged *Egypt*.

The last of the wreckage from over the bullion room was removed on June 9th, when the *Artiglio* went out for the third time that year, and the great day when the diver could direct the grab right into the heart of the bullion had arrived.

Adjoining the bullion room on either side were the mail and baggage rooms. With the bullion room already opened up, it was inevitable that the surge caused by the huge swell of the winter gales would have washed both mail and baggage into the room they had uncovered, but nobody was quite prepared for the mixture which did come up before they caught the first glint of gold.

At first, it was just rubbish—mud, wire, broken pipes, wood and such like. Once, their hopes soared high when one of the crew spotted a piece of wood which could have been part of a box. It bore traces of stencilled letters, but the 'ECTOR' was only part of 'EJECTORS'—there had been a consignment of small arms on board. Then some books, a Port Said cinema programme, bundles of rupee notes, rolls of silk, and several golf clubs. The harvest of rupee notes increased prodigiously in the ensuing weeks, and eventually reached a total face value of the equivalent of over £1,000,000. It was with no little disappointment that they discovered later that the notes were quite worthless as they were. They would have acquired value only by the addition of the facsimile signature of the Hyderabad finance minister.

Success came at long last on June 22nd. Its beginning was modest and unspectacular but exciting enough, and gave everyone a much needed injection of encouragement. The grab could, of course, have come up full of boxes of gold, with perhaps a ton or more worth upwards of £150,000 at that time. Instead, hidden amongst sodden rupee notes, mud and general rubbish, there was just one golden sovereign. For those on the *Artiglio* 'one in a million' had acquired a new and exciting reality.

Before that never-to-be-forgotten day was over, the tiny sovereign had the company of two gold bars and every man on board the little ship genuinely felt that this was indeed the

beginning of the end. That night their celebrations were, however, a mixture of joy and pathos for they remembered in silent
thought those who had been lost in the first *Artiglio*.

All the divers had to do now was to direct the grab into the
bullion room. The weather held fine and in four days almost
one fifth of the *Egypt*'s treasure was lifted out of the wreck and
put into canvas bags on board the *Artiglio*. Then, on Saturday,
June 25th, when a long westerly swell began rolling in and
stopped operations by breaking one of their mooring wires,
Quaglia decided to accept that as a sign that he should set about
delivering his £150,000 cargo. Arrangements had already been
made for this first consignment to be landed at Plymouth, and
it was a proud little ship which steamed past the Eddystone
lighthouse at seven o'clock on Sunday morning, June 26th, 1932.

They were welcomed at Plymouth by an impressive gathering. Mr. and Mrs. Sandberg were there with their two sons.
Count Buraggi, SORIMA's representative, and the Countess,
Sir Joseph Lowrey of the Salvage Association, Mr. Charles de
Rougemont who was one of Lloyds' principal underwriters, and
Sir Percy McKinnon, Chairman of Lloyds—had all come to
greet the *Artiglio*. The Chief Customs Officer was also there, not
to join the others in welcoming the *Artiglio* but to arrest her, in
the name of the Admiralty Marshal. The little treasure-laden
vessel then suffered the indignity of having a writ stuck on her
mast. The warrant had been issued as a result of a claim from
La Société Nouvelle des Pêcheries à Vapeur, the French sub-
contractors who had taken part in the abortive attempt to find
the *Egypt* in 1926. Next morning, however, the gloom was
lifted somewhat by a visit from the Commander-in-Chief
Plymouth, Sir Hubert Brand, and it disappeared completely
that afternoon when the writ was removed from the mast and
news came from London that the bullion had been released.

The midnight train to London on Tuesday June 28th had
coupled to it something unique in the way of parcels vans—one
containing 21 boxes of gold and silver from the sunken *Egypt*.
This first consignment subsequently realized the sum of
£121,924 9s. 9d.

On August 15th the *Artiglio* was back again with another
£81,000 worth. Altogether, she made five trips to Plymouth

that year and her last, on October 14th, when operations were suspended for the winter, brought the total value recovered to over £550,000.

The *Artiglio* resumed work on the Egypt in May 1933 and continued until the end of October, but by then the recovery rate had dwindled considerably. Her fifth and last 1933 delivery to Plymouth on November 3rd, after two months' operations, consisted of only two bars of gold, 21 silver ingots and 490 sovereigns with a total value of less than £8,000 compared with one month's work and a delivery on September 4th of over £61,000 worth.

Towards the end of that season they had found that the deck of the strong room in the wreck had collapsed, scattering the remainder of the bullion and making recovery by grab a difficult and most uneconomical operation.

In 1934 they returned to the job with a new device designed by Mario, who was Quaglia's chief diver on the *Artiglio* at that time, and based on an invention by O. D. Hunt, a British engineer, for the collection of samples from the sea bed. The apparatus, used by the vessel with great success during the latter stages of the recovery operations, comprised a watertight steel cylinder about 14 feet high and nearly 4 feet in diameter. The base of the cylinder was shaped like the bottom of a wine bottle, the top of the indent being sealed only by a glass plate which could be broken by a weight-operated trigger device at the side.

With the air, at normal surface pressure, sealed inside, the cylinder was lowered to the bottom of the gap which had been blasted out of the *Egypt*. The weight in the small tube at the side of the cylinder, which operated the trigger device to break the glass, was controlled from the deck of the salvage vessel. When the cylinder, or vacuum bottle as they called it, was in position for recovery, the weight was dropped and the glass broken.

At the depth at which they were working, the water pressure was nearly twelve times that of the air inside the vacuum bottle, so that when the glass was shattered the sudden inrush of water took with it anything—including gold bars or coins—which happened to be lying there. It proved so successful that operations were continued through the summer of 1934, resulting in the *Artiglio* making three more deliveries to Plymouth. The last, in October, brought the value of the year's recovery of bullion and specie up to a total of £199,910.

The original contract between the Salvage Association and Messrs. Sandberg and Swinburne in 1923, on the basis of 'no cure no pay', provided for the contractors being awarded a certain percentage of the salved bullion. After the second attempt to locate the *Egypt* had failed, the time factor in the agreement was extended and the contractors' proportion increased. In 1928 when SORIMA was engaged, the terms of a new agreement laid down specific percentages for both the contractors and the Italian salvage company, but the stage was reached when it was no longer profitable to continue operations indefinitely.

So it was that, on July 1st, 1935, the *Artiglio* left Brest for her last visit to the wreck of the *Egypt*. The first day of operations, July 4th, ended with the recovery of eight bars of gold and 2,066 sovereigns, a total value of £19,200. Between then and the 12th, when the vacuum bottle went down for the last time, a further 10 bars of gold and 4,918 sovereigns had been brought up, but the last four days bore unmistakable witness to the emptying treasure chest. July 9th had produced one small bar of gold and 454 sovereigns; the 10th, 258 sovereigns only. On the 11th, only 13 sovereigns, and on the 12th—just four.

The 14th and final delivery of the whole operation was made at Plymouth three days later, and was sold for £45,608 17s. 1d.

The salvage of bullion from the *Egypt*, once the wreck had been found, was a most remarkable achievement. The search had cost the lives of brave men and the loss of a ship, but they won through in the end. Their success owed much to the support—both moral and technical—given by Peter Sandberg and James Swinburne, who never allowed their faith in the ultimate outcome of the search and subsequent salvage operations to flag, and rendered invaluable assistance with professional advice on recovery methods and choice of equipment.

Practically the whole of the treasure had been recovered. The little that remained, hidden under the tragic wreck or scattered about the ocean floor and now buried deep and lost for ever under a shroud of sand and mud, should, perhaps, be regarded as a fitting memorial to those who had not lived to share in the final success of the operation.

The degree of that success had been almost unbelievably high—so high, in fact, that the value of the total bullion recovered at 1935 prices greatly exceeded that of the whole shipment in 1922. Nobody could have expected—or dreamed of—or ever hoped for—greater success than that, not even the most optimistic of the underwriters.

CHAPTER NINE

THE *NIAGARA*

When the Royal Mail liner *Niagara* steamed out of the harbour at Auckland, New Zealand on June 18th, 1940, the Second World War was already nine months old but New Zealand's enemy was then on the other side of the world. Japan did not enter the war until nearly eighteen months later. (Plate 10a.)

It was a calm mid-winter evening in Auckland and the war must have seemed a long way away, as indeed it was so far as actual fighting was concerned It was the same for the 148 passengers and 203 crew on the *Niagara*, but for them a hot, tropical summer was only a few days away. They were bound for Suva in the Fiji Islands, 1,100 miles to the north, and then on to Vancouver where another, northern summer would be waiting for them. But they were not to get very far on their journey.

At 3.30 the following morning, June 19th, the *Niagara* passed the Marotiri Islands, six miles to port, and the officer on watch plotted her position. The night was still calm but, by then, bitterly cold. Everybody on board, except those on duty, was sleeping peacefully. Then, at 3.40 a.m. and just ten minutes after passing Marotiri light, there was a shattering explosion. It came from somewhere down below, forward of the bridge. The *Niagara* started settling by the head and listing to port, but fate was kind. She went slowly, and the crew had enough time to get all the boats away.

By 4.45 a.m. the list had increased to about 29 degrees and her fore deck was awash. At 5.30, an hour and twenty minutes after the explosion, the end came. She slid beneath the calm sea and came to rest on the bottom, 440 feet below. Above, under the stars, there was only a great patch of oil, some floating wreckage and the scattered boats. By midday everyone, mercifully, had been picked up by rescue vessels and were later landed at Auckland. A fine ship—grown much in favour with Australians and New Zealanders who had travelled in her during her twenty-seven years of service—had perished.

Unbeknown, and under cover of darkness, a German vessel had sneaked in earlier and sown a minefield in the shipping lane off the east coast of North Island. The *Niagara* was its first victim. She was probably so badly damaged as to be beyond the capacity of ordinary salvage, but her passengers and crew had been saved and that is all which might have mattered. The wreck would have been charted, possibly being marked 'P.A.' —meaning 'position approximate'—and then forgotten, but for the fact that at her previous port of call, Sydney, she had taken on more than just passengers.

Under cover of great secrecy she had loaded a consignment of small, sealed wooden boxes. There were 295 of them, and their total value was about £2,495,700. Those 295 boxes contained about eight tons of gold bars, worth now almost twice that amount. They had been stowed in a locked strong room, four decks down.

The Bank of England had consigned the gold to America where it was urgently needed for war purchases. The Bank of England wanted it back, and took the initiative, which resulted in an expedition under the leadership of Captain J. P. Williams, Managing Director of the United Salvage Proprietary of Melbourne, being organized to attempt recovery.

An old 118-ton coaster, the *Claymore*, was found amongst a bunch of virtual wrecks in Auckland harbour and considered suitable for conversion into a salvage vessel. Her hull had to be patched and her engines put into working order. Anchors and cables, mooring and diving equipment, winches, sweeping gear, fittings and furniture for living and sleeping quarters, galley equipment, a compass, a steering wheel, an engine-room tele-

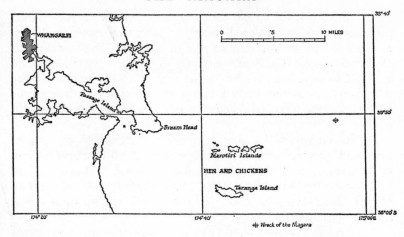

+|+ *Wreck of the Niagara*

graph and a host of other things were needed to replace worn out or missing items. All these had to be begged, borrowed, bought—or otherwise 'found', but in three hectic weeks she was ready with her picked crew of ten men under Captain Williams. His chief diver, John Johnstone, had already achieved some fame by making three descents to a depth of 528 feet, then a world record, and by walking across 27 miles of the Bass Strait between King Island and Tasmania—but not just for fun. The United Salvage Proprietary was surveying the sea bed there in connection with the laying of a submarine telephone cable, and Johnstone was working on it at the time.

The *Claymore* was ready by December 9th, but the Navy was not. Minesweepers were still busy in the shipping lane, and it was the 15th before the little salvage vessel was allowed to begin searching for the *Niagara*. The area to be covered was not large compared with that of other famous searches, and although it was known that the *Niagara* had passed the Marotiri Islands at 3.30 a.m. and would have travelled between two and three miles after that, before striking the mine at 3.40, her movements between then and 5.30 a.m. when she sank could only be estimated. She was known to have her engines at some time during that period, astern as well as ahead, and it was therefore unlikely that she would have maintained her proper course.

When all possible aspects of the crippled ship's movements had been carefully studied, together with the probable effects of the tide at that time, an area of nine square miles north-east of the Hen and Chickens—a group of small rugged islands of which Taranga Island is the 'Hen' and Marotiri Islands are the 'Chickens'—was considered adequate to include all possible positions of the wrecked *Niagara*, and this area was marked with buoys.

An initial survey by echo sounder had revealed nothing of any significance, but it did confirm one very important feature of the search area—the sea bed was reasonably flat. If it had been anything like the top of the adjacent land—Taranga Island rises steeply to over 1,400 feet—the search might well have ended in utter failure.

At first the *Claymore* tried sweeping in a circle round a pivot anchor, but this was soon abandoned for the more effective method of using a pair of sweepers, a small, 10-ton auxiliary, the *Betsy*, having been acquired to assist the *Claymore*. Nine square miles was not the Pacific ocean, but it was large enough for the *Claymore* and the *Betsy*, sweeping at three knots with a wire which spanned a mere 400 to 500 feet of sea bed. Assuming an effective sweeping lane 300 feet wide to allow for overlaps, that meant 180 miles of sweeping.

Time and time again the sweep caught on something, only to come free. Then it had to be hauled in, unravelled, prepared for paying out, and the whole laborious business started all over again. Sometimes the 'something' was a mine and the vessels came near to following the *Niagara* to her watery grave. Once, in late December, they snagged on something which held them fast. The sweep came free but when they got it aboard they found the wire was almost cut through in two places. It had obviously been sawing on something sharp, perhaps the edge of a steep plate. By that time it was dark, and bad weather was blowing up, so the contact was marked with a buoy and both vessels returned to harbour shelter. As soon as the weather improved sufficiently they were out again and, on the 29th, the diver went down in the observation chamber, 408 feet to the bottom. There was a small dark object about 20 feet away from him, but it was too small to be of any significance. It was

Plate 11*a*, £1,340,950 on the hatch of the *Claymore*

Plate 11*b*, 28lb. gold bar caught in teeth of the grab

Plate 12, Composite photo of Comet wreckage

probably just a rock, he thought, and after a good look round he came up. When they hauled in their anchor wire, a mine with its own anchor wire tangled up with theirs came up with it. Discretion was then, obviously, the better part of valour and, wisely, they left the lot where it was for the Navy's mine-sweepers to deal with. The search for the *Niagara* and her gold was not at any time a safe one.

Time and time again bad weather drove them into Whangarei harbour for shelter. Time and time again it seemed that the *Niagara* must have gone down in some other place.

For seven weeks they criss-crossed the area, sweeping first one way and then the other, with the echo-sounder continuously recording the depths. Like Admiral Marten Harperts-zoon Tromp who, some 400 years earlier, was reputed to have 'swept' the seas around England, so Captain John Williams swept the sea bed, there, off Bream Head, and the *Niagara* evaded his 'broom' right through the January of 1941 and into February—but only just. On the afternoon of February 1st the sweep became caught up yet again. The *Betsy* sounded round the spot and found just over 444 feet and then, nearby, the lead struck on something higher. Sounding leads have a hollow bottom which is usually filled with tallow or soap so that a sample of the mud, sand, or shingle, or whatever the surface of the sea bed is composed of, is brought up for more positive identification with the charted soundings in the vicinity. When the lead was pulled up on this occasion there were several flakes of paint on the tallow arming and one of them showed three distinct layers of colour—red lead, grey and buff. The *Niagara*'s paint would have had similar layers, but they had to wait until the following morning to find out whether their search had really ended at last.

Next morning as soon as it was light, the observation chamber was put over and the first thing the diver saw when he reached the bottom was a broken case of tinned fruit. Then he saw some more—in whatever direction he looked, there were boxes of tinned fruit. Not boxes of gold, but still almost worth their weight in that precious metal, for the *Niagara* had indeed been carrying consignments of such a cargo. The *Claymore*, over 400 feet above, moved around so that the diver in the observation chamber could see what else there was in the vicinity, besides cases of fruit. In the dim light he peered and searched, moving a few feet at a time, and then—a grim, battered, 600-foot long mountain of ship showed up in the faint grey-greenness of those deep waters. Their search was over. It was the *Niagara*. The time was 5.10 p.m. on February 2nd, 1941.

Then came the job of laying moorings round the wreck. The *Claymore* had been fitted out with much second-hand gear, for New Zealand was at war and there was a shortage of orthodox mooring equipment. After three of the original improvised moorings had dragged, six-ton concrete sinkers were made to take the place of proper mooring anchors and three-ton blocks of kauri wood were used for buoys. Six moorings were laid at an 800-foot radius from the marker buoy over the *Niagara* and at the hub of that six-spoked wheel—a wire rope to each of the buoys—the *Claymore* took up her position.

After many descents by the diver, the survey of the *Niagara* showed that she was lying on her side at an angle of 70 degrees in soft mud and in 438 feet of water. She bore little resemblance to her former graceful self. Just forward of the bridge there were two gaping holes, one of them 22 feet long and 18 feet across. The forward of her two funnels was no longer there, and about a hundred feet farther aft a great wedge-shaped gash about 45 feet long bore witness to a second explosion, thought afterwards to have been caused by another mine which she had probably struck as she went to the bottom.

Then came the task of blasting through to the bullion in the strong room which was nearly 29 feet from the ship's side, now more horizontal than the deck; but it was nearly nine weeks after the *Niagara* had been found, and April 5th, 1941, before they were ready to start 'digging'. Two weeks had been spent in Whangarei fitting extra lifting gear and winches for operating the grab, and in taking on explosives. The remainder of the time was taken up in surveying the wreck in even greater detail, planning operations—and sheltering from storms, for by March the weather also seemed to be making plans, and even exercising, for its own winter gales.

From careful study of the *Niagara*'s construction drawings and the diver's own survey, a paperboard model of the ship in the

region of the strong room was made by John Johnstone, and
this depicted, in miniature, the tremendous task which confronted them. A hole, something like 60 feet long, 30 feet wide
and 30 feet deep would have to be blasted out of the ship's side,
and the hole cleared of its own 'rubble', before they could get
down into the bullion room. (Plate 10b.)

The first 15 lb. charge was placed on April 5th and by the
21st they were through the hull plating. By May 4th, they were
working desperately through winter's fading light and increasing bad weather, but the hole was now 30 feet long and 12 feet
across, and charges of up to 90 lb. were being used. Thirteen
days later the hole was 40 feet long and 20 feet across and the
deck over the bullion room had been laid bare. At least, it
would have been bare but for the mass of twisted stanchions,
sagging deck plates and tangled steelwork which partly filled
the hole they had, so laboriously, 'dug'.

Blasting was being stepped up all the time and on Monday,
May 19th, over 450 lb. of gelignite was used on that one day.
But the danger now was one of making the charges too big,
which might cause the collapse of the strong room and so make
the precious gold even more inaccessible or, worse still, scatter
it or blow it deeper into the wreck.

Winter gales were causing more and more interruptions and
under-water operations were sometimes impossible for a whole
week. The clearance of débris from the hole was occupying
much of the ever decreasing daylight, but every available hour
was used. On June 1st, the observation chamber was able to get
down right inside the wreck for the first time and although the
strong room was still buried under tons of torn plating and
tangled deckwork, the diver actually caught a glimpse of the
strong room door, 12 feet away.

Clearance of wreckage from the hole, under directions from
the diver in the observation chamber—now that he could
descend into the cavern itself—became more specific, and one
day, the 16th, a great section of 'B' deck plating measuring
about 25 feet by 6 feet was brought up in the teeth of the grab
and dumped clear of the wreck. This sort of grabbing and
dumping made under-water visibility very poor, especially
towards the end of a working day, but sometimes on a fine,

calm, clear morning, the diver could see the whole of the 600-foot long wreck, with the great cavern-like hole yawning black beneath him, as soon as he got below about 360 feet on his first descent of the day.

The bottom of the cavern was now deep down into the ship's accommodation, and, intermingled with jagged steel and splintered wood, there was now tattered clothing, mattresses, blankets, cabin furniture, baths, washbasins, piping and wiring to contend with.

Then followed weeks of grabbing, blasting, clearing, tearing —and then more blasting, right through that mid-winter June, and on through July and the spring of August and September. By then nearly three tons of explosives had been used, and ton after ton of wreckage torn out of the hole. Even when the bulkhead of the strong room was in clear view, a great mass of overhanging deck had to be carefully cut away and removed to make way for the most delicate job of all— that of blasting away the strong room door without doing the same to the boxes of gold inside.

The room itself was nine feet long, six feet wide and eight feet high. Guided as always by directions from the diver in the observation chamber—'Two feet forward', 'Lower bomb', 'Up bomb', 'Two feet to port' and so on—small charges were at last placed on the door hinges. The observation chamber was lifted clear of the water and the charges fired. When the diver went down again he found the door off and lying inside the strong room, on top of the débris. Underneath that débris—the gold.

But first the aperture had to be widened to allow easy entry of the grab. Then, at last, and at 2.30 in the afternoon of October 13th, the ten months of searching, frustration, hopes of success and fears of failure—through a summer, through winter and into summer again, months of blasting and grabbing— all suddenly became worth while. The grab went down, right into the strong room and came up full of wreckage. In the wreckage was one small wooden box, and in the box were two bars of gold, worth together, at that time, nearly £8,500.

On the 15th, the little *Claymore* slipped her moorings and steamed triumphantly into Whangarei harbour. No vessel as

small, or as old, had ever entered Whangarei with greater
pride. Under police escort, the results of her first two days
recovery operations were transferred to the Bank of New
Zealand. There were ten boxes, each weighing 60 pounds, and
the wreck of the *Niagara* was, that day, poorer by £84,600.

The *Claymore* was out again at dawn on Sunday the 19th, and
by 11 a.m. was once more secured in the middle of her wire-
spoked wheel. But maybe the gods were angry with them for
going out after gold on a Sunday—or perhaps just ensuring that
their tremendous success should not go to their heads—for the
next fortnight was bedevilled with setbacks.

When the diver went down on the 19th, as soon as the
Claymore was moored up, he found that he was at least 60 feet
away from the strong room. By the time the ship had been
repositioned and he had been down for another look, the tide
had stirred up the mud and he could not see a thing. Then a
wild, windy night sent the *Claymore* to shelter in the lee of The
Chickens.

Next day the gods relented a little and let them take four
more boxes of gold from the strong room, during a lull in the
weather, but night brought with it a new gale. Two of the
moorings dragged, but they were able to re-lay them next day,
and in the six grab-loads which they achieved before nightfall
they added four more boxes to their precious cargo. That
night, wind and high seas, with violent rain squalls to add to
their discomfort, forced the *Claymore* to slip moorings and return
to Whangarei, but she had another 16 bars—400 lb.—of gold
to prove that the fishing was still good out there.

On the 24th she set out to return to the moorings, but two
hours after leaving Whangarei a rising north-easterly gale drove
her into the anchorage off Passage Island. The 27th rewarded
her with five more boxes—and another north-easterly gale.
She rode out that one—but only just—by slipping from five of
her six moorings. After that, the gods gave them a welcome
break. By November 6th the grab had removed the broken
strong room door, and the total amount recovered had reached
189 bars—over two and a half tons of gold, valued at £810,000.
On the 11th, everyone, including the gods, and everything,
including the weather, seemed to go out of their respective ways

to make it a record day—and record day it was. In six hours of grabbing a total of 46 boxes, nearly £390,000 worth of gold were snatched out.

Up to November 22nd, when a still triumphant *Claymore* went in to Whangarei with her fifth and largest consignment of gold, 205 bars, the rate of recovery, although beginning to waver, had remained high. But it was obvious, with only 34 boxes, or 68 bars, left in the strong room, that the end could not be far away. (Plate 11*a*.)

The original 30-cwt grab, designed to tear out steel wreckage and remove masses of other tangled up débris, had been long since replaced by a smaller one of different design which was better able to scrape up the scraps, but even this was quite unable to get into the corners. What they really needed now was a dust pan and brush, or very large sugar tongs; a diver in an observation chamber, directing a grab in and out of a steel box no larger than a small single bedroom, in semi-darkness and under 400 feet of water, was no substitute.

In any case, nobody was sure that there were still 68 bars there. The under-water lighting only dimly illuminated about six square feet of the strong room and, almost certainly, some of the bars or boxes must have slipped out of the grab on their way up. Diver Johnstone had actually seen one, one day, go flashing past his observation chamber, and he thought the chances of it having fallen back into the strong room were somewhat remote.

Not only was each day's yield getting smaller, but war clouds were already gathering and spreading fast over the darkening skies in the direction of Japan. Any day their peaceful operations might become not quite so peaceful, although it had been far from that on many occasions. Mines had been a grim reminder that war had already stretched its ugly fingers into the very waters that lapped their own still tranquil shores. Most of the reminders had come in the form of explosions, when mines which had been swept up were detonated by the Naval sweepers working off the coast and to seaward of them. Once. when they were in Whangarei for a couple of days, the reminder was a tragic one. The minesweeper *Puriri* struck a mine only two miles from the *Niagara* and lost five of her crew. On another occasion no one needed reminding—it was there for all to see. A mine, tangled up with the *Claymore*'s anchor wire as they were heaving it in, was actually bumping on her bow before it was seen, and most of the crew were taken off while John Johnstone went over in a soft suit to try and unravel the mess. He had barely started when it suddenly shot clear and he found himself, with his own helmet touching the *Claymore*'s bottom, clutching two of the mine's horns with which his own lifeline was entangled. Miraculously he got free and the mine was eventually towed clear without exploding.

After they returned to the wreck on December 3rd they grabbed, and grabbed, and grabbed for four days. On the 4th their 'hook' went down 62 times and only caught a 'fish' twice, but by the morning of the 7th their four days work had been rewarded by a total of 17 bars. Although that represented an average daily return of almost £18,000 they knew that only 35 bars remained—and those 35 could be almost anywhere. That morning, however, it was fine and the water was calm and clear—ideal conditions for a final look round, and so the observation chamber was sent down, right into the opening of the strong room. The steel 'cupboard' itself was quite bare but just outside there was one box resting on a piece of shattered hull plating, and nearby one stray bar scarred with grab marks.

Surely all the gods came to their aid for that last great effort. They needed all the luck in the world to catch those last elusive 'fish', but catch them they did. By the end of the day, with many hours of misses in between, both the box and the bar had been brought up, and the next day, December 8th, 1941, the Bank of New Zealand was presented with the last instalment of 17 gold bars.

It had been an outstanding achievement. Of the original 590 bars entombed in the wreck of the *Niagara*, no less than 555, or 94 per cent had been recovered from the greatest depth ever, and returned to their rightful owners. It was a glorious end but the end had come only just in time. On that same morning came the news of Pearl Harbor, and that New Zealand was at war with Japan.

The prologue and the play were over, but a dramatic

epilogue was still to be enacted. Nearly twelve years later a British salvage company recovered nearly half of the remaining 35 bars of gold, but in the case of one of them—only just. It was caught, almost literally, by the 'skin of its teeth'. (Plate 11*b*.)

CHAPTER TEN

COMET

About 110 miles north-west of Rome and just off the west coast of Italy lies the island of Elba.

For 139 years, up to January 1954, this Mediterranean isle was probably best known as the erstwhile home of the exiled Napoleon, though his stay there had been brief and ended abruptly with his escape in 1815; but before that first month of 1954 was over, Elba was to achieve another distinction—that of having its name given to a Naval operation which was to involve a large number of ships and last for seven months.

The events which resulted in 'Operation Elba Isle' began with the uneventful and routine departure of a Comet aircraft from Rome at 9.31 a.m. on January 10th, 1954. It had come from Karachi via Bahrein and Beirut, and was bound for London. It was a beautiful, sunny morning as the Comet, carrying a crew of six and 29 passengers, took off from Ciampino airport, climbed up through wisps of broken cloud, headed out to sea and then turned north-west, still climbing. Nineteen minutes later, at 9.50 a.m., the aircraft passed over Orbetello beacon, reported to Ciampino Control Tower and flew on towards Elba over which it would have passed on its way to London. It was then approaching 27,000 feet.

One minute after that radio check over Orbetello, the Captain of another BOAC aircraft who had been talking to the Comet heard her Captain say 'Did you get my . . .' when his voice ceased abruptly. That was all he heard, just 'Did you get my'—and then silence. Apart from something unintelligible heard just before ten o'clock by a Ciampino Air Traffic Control clerk who suggested that it might have been an untuned transmission from the Comet, no further signals were received.

Aircraft are usually known by the spoken names of the last two letters of their call signs, the names being taken from the NATO phonetic alphabet, so that Comet G-ALYP was 'Yoke Peter'—but Yoke Peter was no longer flying towards London.

Almost at the same instant that the Air Traffic Control clerk was listening to that last transmission believed to have come from Yoke Peter, people on Elba, 110 miles away from the listener at Ciampino, heard an explosion which seemed to come out of the sky; but it was not until nearly two hours later, at 11.50 a.m., that a report reached the Port Captain at Portoferraio that an aircraft had crashed into the sea to the southward of Cape Calamita and in the direction of the island of Monte Cristo. All available vessels, one of which carried the Port Captain himself as well as a doctor and a nurse, set off immediately to search for survivors, but when they reached the area where the Comet had crashed the doctor and nurse found, tragically, that there was nothing for them to do except help with the dead. All that remained of the 45-ton Comet were pieces of floating wreckage and some mailbags. Of her 35 passengers and crew only 15 bodies were found. There were no survivors.

Aircraft joined in the search which continued for two days, but the sea had given up all that she intended to relinquish at that stage. More floating wreckage was recovered but the remaining dead she kept for ever.

Ten minutes after the Port Captain had been told of the crash, news of the disaster reached both the Ministry of Transport and Civil Aviation and the British Overseas Airways Corporation in London. It was already clear from what had been seen and heard by the local people that Yoke Peter had crashed into the sea at about ten o'clock and that at least part of the aircraft had fallen in flames. When the recovered bodies were brought ashore at Elba and medically examined, it was found that all had burns which had probably occurred after death,

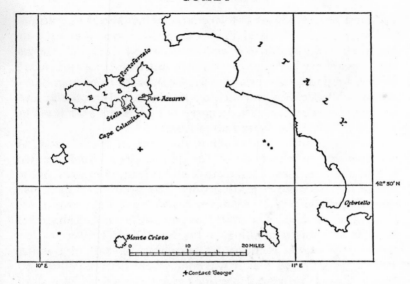

+ Contact 'George'

and that death had been caused by impact with the interior of the cabin. All bore signs, too, of having been subjected to a sudden lowering of atmospheric pressure and to an equally sudden slowing up of movement.

These facts, coupled with the interrupted radio message received by the Captain of the other BOAC aircraft, an Argonaut, had already established beyond doubt that something disastrous had happened with extreme suddenness. This was reflected in the immediate suspension by BOAC of all Comet passenger services and the despatch of orders by the Admiralty to the Commander-in-Chief Mediterranean that an intensive search for the main wreckage was to be organized without delay.

The sea search was soon under way. A Boom Defence vessel, HMS *Barhill* at Malta, was the first to be detailed and started loading up with anchors, cable, wire rope and all the rest of the equipment required for the provision and laying of moorings. A Royal Fleet Auxiliary salvage vessel *Sea Salvor* happened to be on the way from Gibraltar to Malta and was the next ship to be appointed to the search force, which came into tangible being at Malta on January 14th, when Commander Gerald

Forsberg was appointed to take charge of the salvage operations.

The *Sea Salvor* arrived in Malta on the 17th and took on board an under-water television camera and a diver's observation chamber which had been flown out from England. HMS *Wrangler*, a fast anti-submarine frigate, was the third member of the search force. She was already at Malta and left the following day Monday the 18th to carry out an Asdic search of the area in which Yoke Peter had crashed.

There was little doubt about the time of the disaster. A watch found on the body of one of the victims had stopped within a few seconds of ten o'clock and this fitted in with all the rest of the evidence regarding time. The position of the crash was not quite so certain. Eyewitnesses had said that it was to the southward of Cape Calamita, but eyewitnesses' estimates of how far off shore something on fire has fallen into the sea are notoriously vague. Reports by searching aircraft of floating wreckage confirmed that it was somewhere between Elba and Monte Cristo, but actual positions given showed differences of up to ten miles. Two of the boats which had recovered the bodies said that they were south-south-west of Cape Calamita when they had picked them up and that it took them two hours to get back to harbour, but both bodies and wreckage had been drifting for at least four hours when they were first sighted by the boats.

All these different positions made it necessary to establish a search area of about ten miles square and it was in this 100 square miles of ocean floor, most of it between 400 and 550 feet deep, that HMS *Wrangler* commenced looking for the remains of Yoke Peter.

Both the *Barhill* and *Sea Salvor* reached Elba on Monday the 25th, but the weather was far too rough for any sort of salvage operations, and remained so for a whole week—but the week was not lost. Although too bad for laying moorings and investigating contacts already found by the *Wrangler*, the weather did not prevent either ship putting to sea each day to exercise their crews and prepare them for their new and unexpected task. On one of the better days during that week of waiting, the under-water television camera was lowered to a depth of 400 feet and seemed to be functioning perfectly, but it was Sunday,

January 31st before the weather improved sufficiently for them to make a real start. Trawlers were already taking part in the search and trawling over the sea bed in the hopes of scooping up parts of the Comet, when the *Wrangler*'s Asdic made a contact within the search area which justified further investigation. Both *Barhill* and *Sea Salvor* left for the position, *Barhill* to lay moorings and *Sea Salvor* to moor up over the object, send a diver down in the observation chamber and look for the object. If it turned out to be part of Yoke Peter they would endeavour to recover it with the grab.

But a gale intervened once more and it was not until a week later, on the following Sunday, that everything was ready for *Sea Salvor*. Then, secured in the centre of her six-spoked moor, she commenced her search. The diver in his observation chamber hung at the end of over 400 feet of wire rope while *Sea Salvor* above him moved this way and that, a few feet at a time, by adjusting her six mooring wires, with the observation chamber down below swinging into the new position after each move.

Fine weather held for four days while ship and diver moved around within the circle of buoys searching for whatever it was that *Wrangler*'s Asdic had located. At last they found it. Then up came the diver—and *Sea Salvor* slipped from the moorings. That first hopeful object was nothing more hopeful than a bunch of old mine moorings.

HMS *Wrangler* was then relieved by HMS *Wakeful*. In addition to Asdic she also had an under-water television camera. Two more vessels had arrived by Friday the 12th, one of which was the Fleet Tug HMS *Brigand*. She came to deliver three enormous nets each 250 feet long and 50 feet deep. They were made up from wire rope and were to be used to supplement the smaller conventional trawls which, it was hoped, would soon be meeting with some success.

That Friday the 12th was, however, soon to be proved as lucky as Friday the 13th is supposed to be unlucky.

Asdic contacts found by HMS *Wrangler* had been plotted and given names from the same phonetic alphabet which had produced Yoke Peter—'Alpha', 'Bravo', 'Charlie' and so on. Some had been examined and found to be of other than aircraft origin, like the mine moorings which had seemed hopeful enough for a diver's investigation; and on this particular Friday morning HMS *Wakeful* was looking in on her television monitor at contact 'George' and found that George had, indeed, been masquerading under a false name. It was a piece of Yoke Peter, clearly identifiable as such, and at 12.45 the same day the good news that success had come so soon was known by everybody concerned. The Senior Naval Officer (Afloat) Elba had made a signal '*Wakeful* has identified piece of Comet at contact George'.

The position was marked and next day *Sea Salvor* went to examine the area around the find while *Wakeful* and another of the search vessels went off to refuel. With her television camera lowered to within a few feet of the sea bed she moved at snail's pace to and fro over an area of about 900 feet square centred on the piece which *Wakeful* had found. The bottom was littered with pieces of the shattered Comet but all were fairly small. Nothing of any size was sighted. (Plate 12.)

Sunday came and brought with it a sudden gale which sent the search ships into the shelter of Port Azzurro, but *Sea Salvor* was out again on Monday trailing her television camera over the bottom again around contact 'George', but still she found no large sections. HMS *Wakeful* returned on Tuesday the 16th and it was decided that *Barhill* should lay moorings around the patch of wreckage so that some of the pieces could be recovered, but the weather decided to employ delaying tactics once again. It took *Barhill* four days to get all six moorings down. Thursday had been too rough for any of the search ships to be out and they spent the whole of that day anchored in Stella Bay, but Friday was a lucky day again.

By the afternoon it was calm enough for *Sea Salvor* to get on to the moorings and send down the observation chamber. After only a few movements the diver was able to direct the grab on to a piece of aircraft wreckage and minutes later the *Sea Salvor*'s spotless deck was defiled with about five tons of mud, but honoured with one piece of Yoke Peter. Honoured indeed, for history had also been made on that previous lucky Friday, February 12th 1954. Then, for the very first time, under-water television had been used to look at a piece of aircraft on the sea bed 400 feet down, and now that very piece, possibly, was lying on their deck. The position was six miles south of Cape Calamita.

For two days they looked in vain for another piece worth picking up. The see-saw of their luck had gone the other way and stayed there so they tried a new tactic. On Monday the 22nd one of the trawlers was called in to take the end of a long wire rope which had been loaded, in the middle, with a few short lengths of chain. This rather primitive trawl was laid out in as large a circle as possible round *Sea Salvor*; the other end was then passed back on board and the trawl was slowly drawn in, sweeping up whatever lay in its path. At least, that was the idea, and the idea worked—like a magnet. One piece must have attracted another and by the time the loop of the wire had been drawn into the centre of the ring of moorings it was clear, from the increasing weight, that their line had caught quite a lot.

Counting on their luck holding, they lifted their catch until it was to within 20 feet of the surface before sending down a diver to put a proper sling around whatever it was that they had caught, so that it could be hoisted on deck. Their make-shift trawl had fished well. In addition to a seat from the passenger cabin of the lost Comet, there was a mass of electric cable, the after pressure dome and—unexpected and mundane relics from one of the most advanced passenger carrying jet aircraft of its time—both the ladies' and gentlemen's toilets.

Spurred on by the success of their homemade trawl, and to improve its bite, they gave it more teeth in the form of 12 dragging grapnels and repeated their fishing technique on the following day, but without any great success. The 48 hooks only managed to catch one small piece.

Next day, Wednesday, February 24th, they decided to see whether their wire 'broom' had, in its sweeping process, left a pile of bits on the sea floor when it was being lifted. The observation chamber went down and found that it had. By Friday a total of 12 grabfuls of wreckage had been brought up. All of it was from the tail end of the Comet. They knew that the authorities investigating the accident wanted particularly to see the engines, but it looked as though they were somewhere else. Then, before their next move could be decided, the weather broke once again and forced them off the moorings. With a south-westerly gale and a rising sea behind them, they sought the shelter of Port Azzurro. By the time they got out again February had given way to March.

Although the swell left over from the gale made life unpleasant and operations difficult, *Sea Salvor* and *Barhill* working together managed by Thursday of the next week to lay a set of moorings around a new contact, and on the morning of the following day, Friday, March 5th, *Sea Salvor* moored up to look at the object. But the south-west gale had only gone into hiding and no sooner had they got themselves into a position to look than the gale came out again and sent the ships once more into harbour.

Monday, March 8th, saw *Sea Salvor* back on the moorings she had so hurriedly vacated two days before. Two hours later she was preparing to vacate them once more—but not for another gale. The contact had nothing to do with Yoke Peter. It was a sunken dan buoy complete with wire, floats, flag and all. The see-saw of luck was down their end yet again. She stayed and looked during the remainder of the day but there was nothing else there. Another quarter of a square mile of that vast hundred square miles of ocean floor had been pronounced clear and search for the remainder of Yoke Peter went on.

HMS *Whirlwind* was now the other television carrier, in place of *Wakeful*, and joined in the hunt while trawlers continued with their trawling. By Thursday the 11th there was only one plotted contact left which was considered worth examining.

Barhill struggled through a rising south-easterly wind to get moorings down, and then *Sea Salvor* spent the next two days wondering whether to hang on grimly in the hope that the weather would improve or to admit defeat and go back into harbour again. She chose the former of the two alternatives—and won.

On Monday the 15th conditions were just good enough by midday for the observation chamber to go down and then, almost at once, the diver found himself looking at a huge piece of the Comet which was grabbed without much difficulty and hoisted up on deck. It was the centre section of Yoke Peter and through it ran the rear of the two wing spars. It was 65 feet long. Down went the diver again and saw still more. The next grab brought up the front spar from the wing, which was even longer than the rear one. Two of the engines were down there too; the diver had seen them, but with the great torn and jagged centre section and wing spars sprawled across the deck they could take no more. Before slipping, all the mooring wires were marked and a buoy laid, as additional guides to mooring up the next day. They wanted to be sure of getting back into exactly the same position.

Having delivered her very important pieces of cargo, *Sea Salvor* was back on the job by 11 o'clock next morning but when the observation chamber went down the diver saw absolutely nothing—except the bottom. In spite of all the careful marking, the ship was not, obviously, in exactly the same position. When the spokes of a wheel are 2,000 feet long and consist of wire rope and chain, the hub can easily be a little out of centre especially when it is floating in 400 feet of water, and the hub in this case was the *Sea Salvor*. After moving slowly around all the afternoon it was after 5 o'clock when the diver, guiding the grab to pick up quite a small piece of fuselage, found himself almost on top of one of the engines.

The good weather held, and by the Friday evening they had brought up the second engine and both found and recovered the port and starboard undercarriages as well as more of the fuselage. There were plenty of smaller pieces still scattered about but nothing, after that, that the trawlers could not cope with. So the moorings were lifted and trawlers came in to gather up the gleanings. In eight days, from the 21st to the 29th, they worked in and around the area and were richly rewarded with a wide variety of bits and pieces from the wrecked Comet, and also with one which was neither just a bit nor a piece. The trawlers, at least, were rewarded by netting it. The *Sea Salvor* brought it up. But meanwhile, Comets had started to fly again. Although the precise cause of the accident was not yet known, a committee consisting of representatives of BOAC, the Air Registration Board and de Havillands, the designers and builders of the Comets, had considered every possible failure which could have conceivably resulted in an accident of that nature and drawn up a list of tests and appropriate modifications designed to prevent any repetition of such failures. By March 23rd these modifications had been incorporated in all Comet I aircraft and permission was given for flights to be resumed; but efforts to recover still more of Yoke Peter—efforts to find out for certain what had caused the disaster—continued without respite.

The fishing boats had trawled up instruments, engine parts, pieces of the tail plane and more of the main wing. Four times during those eight days of trawling around that same area their trawls got caught up by something down there on the bottom, and that something was large and heavy enough to resist the trawlers' efforts to move it. In view of other recoveries in the vicinity it could not be left in doubt and so, on Tuesday, March 30th, moorings were laid around this so far unidentified object. Some time before, one of the trawlers had lost her net in that area; it carried away after she had snagged on something. Perhaps this was that 'something'.

On March 31st, *Sea Salvor* moored up and the observation chamber went down. Sea conditions were good. The swell which had been making it awkward for the trawlers had died away and when the observation chamber reached the sea bed the diver found that under-water visibility was good, too; better in fact than it had been at any time since the start of the search. Even down there, over 400 feet from real daylight, he could see for about 25 feet, and at the end of an hour's moving about he saw, not the object, but that an object was there. What he did see was that something large was completely enveloped in a heap of trawl net.

Under his direction, the chamber was moved closer and then slowly around it while he tried to get a glimpse of what was underneath. After half an hour of this submarine hide-and-seek he could see that it was undoubtedly some part of a large aircraft, which was all they wanted to know. The observation chamber had been so close to the pile of net that, when it came up after the grab had been lowered into position, the chamber brought the net with it.

After what seemed an age, the grab and its precious load

was brought up through that 420 feet of water and then the great iron mouth deposited on the deck the largest piece of Yoke Peter so far recovered. It was the whole of the forward section from nose to wing, with all the vital controls and the instrument panel complete.

Now that the main sections had been found, there was little likelihood that any of the remaining wreckage could not be adequately dealt with by the trawlers and so, after recovery of the forward part of Yoke Peter, *Sea Salvor* and the other naval ships cleared up their base in Elba and said goodbye to Operation Elba Isle.

In less than three months much of the wrecked aircraft, which had been scattered over the ocean floor south of Elba, had been found, brought up from 400 feet and more and flown home for examination by the Royal Aircraft Establishment at Farnborough, where experts were gradually reconstructing the shattered Yoke Peter from the various parts which had been recovered.

Back in the Mediterranean, 800 miles from Farnborough, trawlers continued with their sweeping. There were parts of Yoke Peter still missing which might provide the answer, but long before the part which really did that was found, disaster struck the ill fated Comets yet again.

On April 8th, the day before *Sea Salvor* sailed for Malta, Comet G-ALYY—Yoke Yoke—on a routine passenger flight from London to Cairo, took off from Ciampino Airport, Rome at 6.32 p.m. Like the rest of the Comets she had been grounded after the accident to Yoke Peter and then returned to service after all the checks had been made and all the agreed modifications incorporated. With a crew of six but carrying only 14 passengers, she climbed up through layers of cloud to the clear cold air above, flew out to sea and then turned south-east towards the toe of Italy. Twenty-five minutes later and still climbing she passed Naples 40 miles away on her port beam and reported to Ciampino. At 7.5 p.m. just over half an hour after take-off and then approaching 35,000 feet, Yoke Yoke spoke to Cairo, announcing her departure from Rome and giving her estimated arrival time at Cairo, and then—silence. Complete and frightening silence.

All attempts to re-establish radio contact were unsuccessful and when she failed to arrive at Cairo there was only one explanation. Next morning, HMS *Eagle* and *Daring*, which happened to be in the area, were ordered to search along the intended flight track of the Comet from her last known position. Aircraft from HMS *Eagle* flew off to widen the field of search and United States aircraft joined in. About 40 miles north of the Strait of Messina they found bodies and floating wreckage. A few aircraft passenger seats, six bodies, and some other pieces of aircraft wreckage were all that were ever recovered. They were identified as having come from Yoke Yoke and closer examination some time later confirmed BOAC's worst fears. There was not a shred of evidence to suggest that the same disastrous failure had not caused the destruction of both Yoke Yoke and Yoke Peter, and all Comet services were once more immediately suspended.

The prospects of recovering more of Yoke Yoke from the sea bed were so remote that no attempt was made to do so. Where the aircraft had crashed the sea was well over half a mile deep, between 3,100 and 3,500 feet.

This second disaster, coming as it did while the cause of the first was still a matter of conjecture, made further recoveries of wreckage from Yoke Peter even more imperative. At the same time the Ministry of Supply ordered RAE to proceed with the fullest possible investigation of the problem now created by the occurrence of two accidents involving identical aircraft, both of which had met with disaster over the central Mediterranean under similar conditions and in almost identical circumstances. Both had occurred within a minute or two of half an hour after take off and when the aircraft were nearing the top of their climb.

The fact that Yoke Yoke had crashed in spite of all the modifications which were incorporated following the disaster to Yoke Peter enabled many of the original possible causes of failure to be ruled out, and attention became directed towards the possibility of failure of the pressurized cabin. It was for this reason that Operation Elba Isle was continued and search extended south-eastwards along the flight path of Yoke Peter. The bursting of the cabin, if such was the cause, probably resulted in some part of it being blown clear and falling some distance away from where the main sections had been discovered.

The Italian fishing boats trawled on and found more wreckage. On May 7th the starboard outer wing was trawled up. Later in the month the tail unit was recovered, and during June another piece of the centre fuselage and the fin were found. Then, on August 12th, trawling in ever deepening water south-eastwards along the flight track, one of the boats found a piece of wreckage which was later identified by RAE as coming from the top of the cabin above the front of the two wing spars and including both of the windows which contain the Automatic Direction Finding aerials. This portion reached Farnborough on the last day of August, about the same time as parts of the port wing aileron and leading edge nearer the wing tip.

These three pieces provided remarkable evidence that a catastrophic bursting of the cabin had occurred in the region of the front spar and during otherwise normal flight. Microscopic examination of marks on the wing parts proved that they had been caused by pieces of the cabin, and on the leading edge of the wing they had found the impact mark of the fractured edge of a blue band painted on the outside of the cabin wall.

The long months of searching and finding had been worth while. The answer had been trawled up from the ocean floor.

By then the last recovery had been made. On August 21st the outer part of the port tail plane was picked out of the trawl of one of the boats. It was, perhaps, a fitting finale that the recovery of this tail end piece also marked the end of seven months search, and Operation Elba Isle took its honoured place in the history of salvage from the sea.

About 70 per cent of the aircraft had been found and lifted from the ocean floor, and the evidence resulting from expert examination of the wreckage by RAE had enabled a vivid picture to be built up of the last few moments of that disastrous flight.

A structural failure of the pressurized cabin due to fatigue had caused the accident and the wreckage had provided irrefutable evidence of the manner in which the Comet had broken up and crashed. The first fracture of the cabin had occurred at one of the forward corners of the rear ADF aerial windows. Following the sudden bursting of the structure, the aircraft was subjected to a terrific downward force and the after part of the fuselage, complete with the tail unit, fell away. At the same time the outer portions of the wings and the complete nose section left the main part of the wing which then caught fire and burned for about three minutes, the time taken for this centre section to reach the sea from a height approaching 30,000 feet. It then turned right over, with the engines stopped, and hit the sea upside down. The tail end continued its downward plunge and entered the sea open end first.

All this and much more was established by expert study of the parts which had been recovered. It was almost as if they had been able to re-enact every second of those last fearful three minutes.

Another Comet—Yoke Uncle—was pressure-tested in a water tank and subjected to stresses which simulated 1,830 pressurized flights before the cabin structure failed, but when it did so the failure started at the corner of one of the cabin windows. No efforts were spared to find out what had gone wrong and what was needed to prevent its recurrence, and tests carried out with a light wood scale model of a Comet which was designed to break up like Yoke Peter—and at a height and speed corresponding proportionately with those at which the aircraft was flying at the time of the disaster, with the pieces being photographed all the way down and into the water—produced evidence which supported much of what had previously been little more than conjecture.

The searching, the finding and the scrupulous investigation was all worth while. As a direct result of the tragic loss of the two Comets and the subsequent enquiries which spared no effort to arrive at a satisfactory conclusion, many constructive measures which raised the standard of British aircraft to an even higher level and substantially improved both the efficiency and safety of air travel were adopted—and the Comet flew again.

CHAPTER ELEVEN

VICTOR

About 18 miles westward from St. Ann's Head at the entrance
to Milford Haven on the Pembrokeshire coast of Wales stands
the Smalls lighthouse, towering 126 feet above a patch of rocks
which are just awash at high water.

Over England and Wales August 20th, 1959 was a fine sunny
day, but out in the Irish Sea and St. George's Channel there
were extensive fog patches. At about 11.40 that morning, west
of the Smalls, a southbound coaster ran out of the fog into clear
weather, and the conspicuous red and white bands of the lighthouse stood out in the bright sunlight, six miles away on her
port bow. Suddenly, a little on her starboard bow, what
appeared to be two dark columns of water rose out of the sea.
They were some distance away but near enough for the officer
on watch to see a taller column of spray shoot up from between
them. The spray seemed to hang in the air as if it was suspended
from above and then, a few seconds later, came a double
explosion. To those on board the coaster, the splash appeared
to be beyond their visible horizon. It was estimated to be about
eight miles west of the Smalls and about 50 feet in height.

The coaster called Ilfracombe radio station and reported the
splash and explosion, but the incident had occurred in an area
covered by an experimental missile range and no great importance was attached to it at that time. The radio station said
'Thanks very much, old man', or words to that effect, and the

coaster went on its way. The only record of the occurrence to be made that morning was a brief entry in the vessel's log.

Those on board little knew, then, that the splash they had seen and the entry in the log were to become vital evidence in a search which was to involve dozens of ships and more than a thousand men, in an operation which was to dwarf even the Comet search off Elba in 1954.

On that morning of August 20th the prototype Victor Mark 2 bomber had left Boscombe Down airfield in Wiltshire on a flight across the Pembrokeshire coast and out over the Irish Sea. It was a routine flight—but one from which she was destined never to return.

Shortly after midday, lack of communication from the Victor gave rise to fears for her safety and a few hours later a BBC radio announcement made it known that an aircraft was overdue from a flight over the Irish Sea. The announcement was heard by the coaster which immediately contacted the shore station again, and within minutes Boscombe Down knew of the vessel's earlier report.

The estimated position of the splash was too near that of the last plot of the aircraft to be ignored, and when it was found that the Victor could well have been in that place at that time, there remained no doubt about the significance of the information.

Coastal Command Shackletons, naval ships, helicopters and a lifeboat were called out immediately and started an intensive search over the sea, while coastguards and troops searched ashore, looking for anything which might yield a clue to what had happened to the £2,500,000 'V' bomber and her missing crew of four RAF officers and chief test observer from Handley Page, the builders of the Victor.

Days went by. Reports of floating wreckage and oil slicks were investigated but nothing was found. Then, on August 26th, six days after the aircraft had disappeared, a boy on holiday down on the beach at Porthmelgan, a tiny cove near St. David's Head, saw a piece of something white floating in the sea a few yards off shore. He knew about the search for the missing aircraft and so he waded in and pulled the piece of wreckage ashore. It looked like a piece of an aircraft, he thought, and took it to St. David's coastguard station. Within hours it had

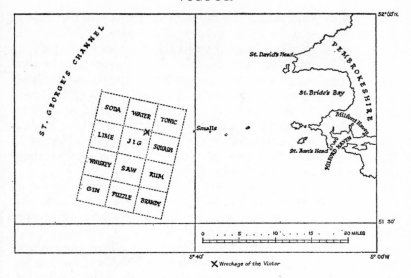

X Wreckage of the Victor

been identified by Boscombe Down as a piece of the lost Victor.

Four days later, and ten days after the plane had vanished, troops were searching along 130 miles of the Welsh coast and a RAF mountain rescue team were combing the mountains inland, the discovery of a piece of flying helmet and portions of the Victor's radar dome on shore having raised hopes that some of the crew had baled out over the land or that it was only part of the aircraft which had fallen into the sea. Holidaymakers and local residents joined in, and men from a Royal Naval Air Station, using boats, searched coves under the 200 foot cliffs.

But the sea, nearly 400 feet deep where the splash had been seen, was the main objective and on August 31st, after a RAF launch had taken samples of oil from a patch sighted 14 miles off the coast by a Shackleton, four naval frigates, a naval salvage vessel equipped with under-water television, and two Milford Haven trawlers began a systematic search of an area 12 miles wide by 16 miles long around the estimated position of the splash seen by the coaster.

For the Operations Room Staff at HMS *Harrier*, the naval shore station controlling the search operation, and for the ships' crews station controlling the search operation, and for the ships' crews, that stretch of water south-west of the Smalls ceased overnight to be just part of St. George's Channel. Instead, a particular position was said to be in area 'Jig', or 'Saw' or 'Puzzle', in 'Water', 'Soda' or 'Whiskey'. Twelve areas, each four miles square, made up that 192 square miles of search area and each one was given a code name. 'Jig', 'Saw' and 'Puzzle', in that order, were the most hopeful areas and north of 'Jig' was area 'Water'. These were flanked by 'Soda', 'Lime', 'Whiskey' and 'Gin' to the west and 'Tonic', 'Squash', 'Rum' and 'Brandy' to the east, names which suggest that they originated in the Ward Room of HMS *Harrier*.

A whole month went by, a month of glorious summer weather during which naval vessels swept the sea bed with Asdic. As contacts were found each one was given a name, using the NATO phonetic alphabet, 'Alpha', 'Bravo', 'Charlie', 'Delta' and so on, and carefully plotted by the ships and the Operations Room staff ashore. By the end of September they were up to 'Romeo' but still nothing had been actually found—nothing except the 24 small pieces of the bomber's radar dome which had been picked up along the Pembrokeshire beaches, mostly in St. Bride's Bay, and the piece of flying helmet.

By the time 'Romeo' was added to the list, more than half of the previous ones had already been eliminated after further investigation. 'Bravo' had turned out to be a hitherto uncharted rock peak nearly 100 feet high. 'Foxtrot', 'Lima', 'Oscar' and some of the others were boulders, or dense shoals of fish—or could not be found a second time. 'Hotel' was an old wreck, but 'Delta' was still there and seemed to be about the right height and size according to the echo sounder and Asdic traces. It was to be investigated as soon as possible.

Half a dozen naval vessels, two steam trawlers and a couple of seine-net fishing boats were still sweeping the 192 square miles of search area as September drew to a close.

The salvage vessel *Twyford*, chartered by the Admiralty, had now joined the search force. She was fitted with Asdic, a heavy lift derrick, huge grabs capable of several tons at a time and deep diving equipment. She laid six moorings around contact 'Delta' and prepared to investigate. It was exactly a month to the day since the Victor disappeared, but the fine weather was beginning to break and next morning, before anything further could be attempted, a 27-knot wind and rising sea forced her to slip from the moorings.

By September 28th, after 'Delta' had been repositioned by Asdic, the heavy moorings shifted one by one to encircle the new position, and hours of searching by a diver in an observation chamber suspended just above the sea bed on 300 feet of wire rope, this most hopeful of all the contacts so far was found to be nothing more than a mound of rock and boulders. One more contact had been eliminated.

Meanwhile, 14 miles away, outside the search area proper but very close to the spot where the oil slick had been sighted a month earlier, one of the seine-net fishing boats had 'snagged' —that is, her net had caught on something on the sea bed and held her fast. The position was also very near contact 'Romeo' which was still unconfirmed, and so near in fact that it was thought that the seine-netter might have snagged on 'Romeo' itself. The *Twyford* was called in to lay moorings and investigate.

As soon as she was in position, down went the observation chamber. The water, near the bottom, was thick with plankton, and even with three 1,000-watt lights shining down from just above the observation chamber, the diver inside could see little of the sea bed below him. The chamber was brought up and one of the naval Asdic ships was summoned to assist. She laid off, a few hundred yards away, pinging with her Asdic both the contact on the sea bed and the *Twyford* above, noting the range of each.

"Move twenty yards to starboard" came her order over the radio telephone. Then "Another ten", and after that "Thirty yards astern", and now *Twyford* was right over the contact. Down went the huge grab and landed open on the bottom, then slowly closed and heaved up. As it broke surface, water and mud streaming out from between its eight legs, all eyes were fixed on it but the huge claws had closed on no wreckage—only gouged out a ton of sea bed. After a three yard move to port they took another grab at whatever was down below, but again it was only sea bed which came up. Then more moves and more sea bed. Tides were beginning to run fast, for the top of Springs was only two days off. Operations were temporarily suspended.

While the *Twyford* was in Milford Haven during the spring tides she had a Pye underwater television set installed on board, and when operations were resumed on October 7th she was ordered to lift the 'Romeo' moorings so that the seine-netters could sweep through the area and re-locate the contact. There followed three days of fruitless shooting and hauling of nets and then a south-easterly gale sent the whole of the search force back into harbour for shelter. The following Tuesday, October 13th, one of the seine-netters found and buoyed 'Romeo' again. Once more the naval Asdic vessel positioned the *Twyford* right over the contact. Yes, it was there all right, and so moorings were laid and the search started again, but now they had their under-water television to help.

Down went the camera, but the plankton was still thick and looking at the television monitor on the bridge was like looking through a small window at thick fog and driving snow outside. It was still the same next day, so they resorted to grabbing again but nothing but clay and rocks came up. Two hours and ten moves later, and over the radio telephone from the Asdic ship still pinging the *Twyford*, her grab and 'Romeo' itself from 600 yards away came the message "You have cut Romeo in half—we are getting two contacts now, with a small gap in between".

The mystery of 'Romeo' was solved. It was a short, high ridge of clay and rocks, and *Twyford* had bitten out the middle.

Up came the moorings once more, and up came the gales too. It was Friday the 23rd before operations were resumed and then, 14 miles north-west from 'Romeo', 'Sierra' was found and buoyed. One of the trawlers had snagged and cut one of her net warps right through, and the frayed end bore traces of something white. The Victor was mainly white, and within hours the precious sample of rope had been collected and was on its way by helicopter to RAE Farnborough for examination.

Weeks went by, and gale followed gale. In between, a few days at a time, searching—Asdic sweeping—echo sounding—trawling. Only ten days in October were good enough for operations. For over half of November the whole search force was weather-bound in Milford Haven. December opened with more gales and the first one, on the 2nd, was fierce enough to send the *Twyford* to Barnstaple Bay, 75 miles to the south-east, for shelter. On the 8th, while sheltering in Milford Haven from another gale, some of the ships were nearly blown out to sea again by a 55-knot wind.

By then, 'Sierra' had turned out to be a mountain of sea urchins. The dense mass had cut through the trawler's warp and the laboratory staff at RAE Farnborough had found they were analysing sea urchin instead of white paint. 'Tango' had been found, 7 miles south-west of the Smalls and right on the line of bearing of the splash seen by the coaster three months earlier, and it took the *Twyford* ten days to complete the investigation of what proved to be nothing more than an isolated patch of large boulders.

December had given the ships only six days of weather suitable for searching and then, after the Christmas break, it was January 4th before they could put to sea again.

Next day a Milford Haven trawler, out fishing, hauled in her net at the end of a 12-mile trawl. She was then ten miles south-west of the Smalls. She had a moderate catch and among the fish was a crumpled piece of metal, silvery white, about 18 inches by 12 inches. Her skipper knew the Milford Haven trawlers engaged on the Victor search and called one of them by radio and told him of his find. By the following morning everyone in the search force knew that RAE Farnborough had identified the piece of metal as part of the Victor.

At last the sea had revealed her secret, hidden until now for four and a half months. At last they all knew for certain that the aircraft, or part of it, was down there—somewhere. But where? Where, in that 12-mile long trawl, had the piece been scooped up? Had some other trawler dragged it along with her trawl warp, only to drop it again somewhere in that 12 mile lane which ended just inside the search area? The *Twyford* was called in to Asdic-sweep along the line of trawl and for one and a half miles on either side of it—another 36 square miles of searching.

On the fringe of the three mile wide lane and two and a half miles east of the start of the trawl, *Twyford* had a contact. Careful investigation by Asdic and echo sounder indicated wreckage about 15 feet high and their hopes rose—this new one, 'Uniform', might be part of the crashed Victor. Moorings were laid on January 12th and as soon as *Twyford* was in position right above the wreckage, down went the television camera, but near the bottom it was still like a snowstorm in thick fog. Then the camera struck something hard and all the lamps shattered. It was obviously too dangerous to send the observation chamber down in those conditions and so they rigged the large grab. On the echo sounder they saw it go down and land on the contact.

It came up, a mass of rusty tangled wreckage in its claws—and 'Uniform' was eliminated, for the wreckage, a bunch of ironwork which once had been steel frames and shell plating, was obviously that of a small ship. It was probably a First World War casualty which had lain there, unknown and undisturbed, for more than 50 years until the searchers for the wreckage of an aircraft such as could not have been even dreamed about by the crew of that ship tore a piece from her rusting skeleton.

The weather was worsening rapidly and *Twyford* slipped from the buoys. Forty-eight hours later all the ships were back in harbour and a north-easterly gale was sweeping the Irish Sea. It was Sunday, January 17th before they were able to lift the moorings from around 'Uniform'.

More Asdic-sweeping—more trawling—more snags with negative results—and January, which had given them 18 more days at sea, slipped into February with the mystery of the Victor bomber a greater mystery than ever, when one of the seine-net boats working nine miles south-west of the Smalls, right on the 'Jig'–'Lime' boundary and only one and a half miles from the end of 12-mile trawl line, found in her net a small piece of fibre glass. It was flown to Farnborough and assessed as 'almost certainly of Victor origin'.

At that time five ships were working in that area and then, three miles south of where the piece of fibre glass had been recovered and less than half a mile from the 'farthest away possible' position of the—by now almost mythical—splash, one of the trawlers became caught up on something. The weather was deteriorating rapidly and she could not recover her trawl. The *Twyford* was Asdic-sweeping a few miles to the north and was ordered by radio to go to her assistance, but by the time she arrived the wind was gusting to 38 knots. Fearing the trawler might part her warps and so lose the whole of her trawl as well as the position of the snag, *Twyford* dropped a marker buoy on the spot—but only just in time. Within minutes of the marker buoy going over, both of the trawl warps parted and her gear went to the bottom. Nothing more could be done and all ships set course for Milford Haven, 30 miles away, with a south-west gale behind them.

As soon as the *Twyford* put to sea again she carried out both an Asdic and echo-sounder survey around the position but without results. Then the seine-netter came in again, and after three days of sweeping with a grapnel picked up the trawl warp and passed it over to the *Twyford* to heave in by hand. After hours of careful hauling, a few feet at a time, in came the net. It was badly torn but had nothing in it except an old tin can, but the marker buoy was right on the spot and *Twyford* was ordered to 'lay moorings, investigate and recover'.

The sea remained too rough for diving, and *Twyford* kept off the moorings while trawlers went through to re-locate the contact. For a second time it was caught up in a trawl which carried away a few minutes later, just after the marker buoy had been dropped. Then, after shifting all six moorings so as to encircle the new position more accurately, *Twyford* moored up. A welcome spell of really calm weather made it possible to use the observation chamber, and after four hours of searching the diver spotted the trawl warp lying on the bottom. Slowly, six feet at a time, under directions from the diver, the salvage vessel above carried the observation chamber back along that thin brown 'worm' stretching away in tantalizing curves across the sea bed. Yard by yard they tracked it, sometimes losing it for several moves. For hours the diver traced it back towards the net end, and then at midnight with a 25-knot beam wind straining their weather side wires to near breaking point, the *Twyford* was forced to slip from the buoys.

Early next afternoon she was back on the moor, but although the wires had been carefully marked before they let go the previous day, another five hours of searching the sea bed ended without finding the rope again. Next day, after four more hours of tedious searching, the rope was again spotted by the diver and late that night they were still tracking it, but by then the

ship was close up to one of the mooring buoys and could go no
farther. The grab was lowered, positioned by the diver and
came up with the bight of the trawl warp in its claws. Just
before midnight the net was recovered—empty.

Those on the *Twyford*, and on the other ships, were beginning
to wonder if it was the gremlins at work down there, thousands
of them hanging on to a trawler's net until she was stopped and
then, when the marker buoy sinker came down, rolling a rock
on to the net and then rushing away laughing—to find another
trawl.

The operations staff ashore must have been thinking along
similar lines, for Naval Control decided that these mysterious
snags were too mysterious to be given so much importance
unless supported by other evidence, and on March 8th *Twyford*
was ordered to recover the moorings from 'Whiskey'. Normally,
'Victor' would have followed 'Uniform' but for obvious
reasons was reserved for use later.

The investigation of 'Whiskey' had lasted for six weeks, and
those six weeks of operations—interrupted five times by gales
and a total of 13 days in harbour for bad weather—had done
little to suggest that success was anywhere near.

On Sunday March 13th, the largest of the search force
trawlers was working in area 'Jig', and was about seven and a
half miles south-west of the Smalls when she hauled at the end
of her run. In her trawl were four pieces of bent and twisted
metal, some pieces of fibre glass and a few lengths of plastic
covered wire. Fourteen objects in all which, next day, were
identified by RAE Farnborough as wreckage from the Victor
bomber. Seven months of searching and at last, from within
the known limits of an organized and plotted trawl line, pieces
of the Victor had been recovered. At last they had a position
from which to work.

A few more small pieces were recovered a mile or so to the
north while the *Twyford* carried out an echo-sounder survey of
three square miles of sea bed, centred seven miles west of the
Smalls and embracing the two positions where the wreckage
had been recovered. The bottom was found to be reasonably
flat and smooth and the depth varied only between 377 feet
and 383 feet. It was good ground for trawling for aircraft

Plate 13*a*, a Pye TV screen shows wreckage
of *Victor*

Plate 13*b*, Part of *Thresher* photographed
by bathyscaph *Trieste*

Plate 14a,
Redesigned
bathyscaph *Trieste II*

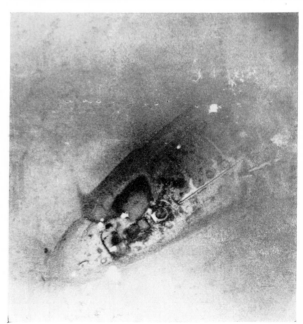

Plate 14b,
USS *Scorpion*
photographed on
ocean floor by
USNS *Mizar*

wreckage and three trawlers were brought into the area. They worked throughout the night in deteriorating weather and at 10 o'clock next morning they were forced to give up, but by then they had on board 31 pieces of Victor, including part of an engine.

By Saturday the 26th more engine parts and a whole ejector seat had been recovered, and the total had grown to 87 pieces of wreckage. The almost forgotten splash at last began to have some significance, for its first estimated position was not very far from where the wreckage was now being found.

The main task, now, was trawling for more wreckage, and by carefully regulating the length of the trawlers' runs and evaluating and plotting every haul the operations room staff ashore were able to build up a picture of the wreckage scatter. By April 4th a total of 275 pieces had been recovered and the plot was beginning to take shape. On the 7th the ships were given a position which the plot showed to be the centre of the wreckage concentration, and on that spot—Green Juliet 32.95 Purple India 64.35, the Decca Navigator readings of the position—the *Twyford* dropped a marker buoy. Around that buoy, at a radius of 400 yards, she laid her six moorings.

Before running out wires to the buoys the marker had to be lifted. This operation followed the usual routine procedure without much interest—but only at first. Just before the sinker appeared a great shout of triumph went up from the watching crew, for there—tangled up in the sinker wire—were two small twisted pieces of metal and several feet of fine steel wire. The metal was aircraft wreckage, and the steel wire, too. It was Victor wreckage. After nearly seven months of monotonous searching, all through that wild winter, the *Twyford* had recovered her first piece—at last.

As soon as she was moored, down went the television camera —but fate was laughing at them again, for again it was thick 'fog' down there on the bottom, but in this case it was not plankton. That was higher up—the camera had passed through the plankton layer on the way down and this was just dirty water. Into the south Irish Sea and St. George's Channel the south going tidal stream carries with it all the waste water from the sinks and bathrooms and gutters of Dublin and Blackpool, of

Belfast and Liverpool, while the north going stream brings in clean water from the Atlantic. They had found, over the months, that a north going stream gave much better sea bed visibility and so they decided to wait until the tide turned. In the afternoon, as soon as the north going stream was well under way, they put the observation chamber over, and almost before it had steadied in position, a few feet from the bottom, the diver reported pieces of aircraft wreckage in sight. Thursday, April 7th, was indeed their lucky day.

Taking advantage of the good sea bed visibility and blessed with a spell of fine weather, they devoted the rest of the day, right on until nearly midnight, to moving about and seeing what was down there. There was no doubt about it. Mangled, torn and twisted wreckage of the crashed Victor bomber lay scattered about on the sea bed beneath them. In the first hour the diver sighted between 60 and 70 separate pieces. The largest was about six feet long and two feet wide, and the smallest a tiny fragment of metal three inches by one inch, shining like a mirror under the light from the three 1,000-watt lamps above the observation chamber.

The *Twyford* moved around within the moor, and the observation chamber moved around with her. "I'm over a heap of it" came the diver's voice out of the amplifier in the wheelhouse, "about three feet high. Just a pile of it, about ten feet one way and six feet the other. Looks as if it had been swept up together and just left here." Perhaps, they thought, this had been one of the contacts, gathered up in a trawl some time and just emptied out there as the bottom of the net split open by the sheer weight of it—or maybe the gremlins, with brooms.

Just after midnight, at the end of that memorable day, a glorious afternoon and now a brilliant, cloudless moonlit night, they put the grab over and, under the diver's directions, brought up two grabsful of wreckage. The first load included a piece of engine, part of a wing structure, lengths of electric wire, and 83 small pieces. The largest piece in the second grabful was ten inches long.

The cloudless, moonlit night disappeared long before dawn and another south-west gale was threatening, but by 7 o'clock the chamber was over again. Their luck was out. The south going stream was bringing down the dirty water again, and the tide—assisted by the rising wind on their port quarter—had moved the *Twyford* from where she had been, tightly moored, the night before. Not one piece of wreckage was in sight. It was half past ten, after over 70 movements had been carried out, before any was seen—and then only one grabful of nothing much was achieved before operations had to be suspended.

The underwater television camera had already been fitted to the top of the smallest grab, which had the effect of giving the camera a set of claws. Later on they made several attempts with that, but only succeeded in dumping a lot of mud on the deck and after a fruitless and frustrating afternoon's work they gave it up for the day.

By daylight next morning the wind was up to 30 knots. They slipped the bow wires, but then the wind took charge and carried away the rest of the moorings. All ships returned to harbour—with the first consignment of Victor bomber.

Trawlers recovered more than a thousand pieces before the *Twyford* was able to get back on to the moorings the following Tuesday, and although it was then after 8 o'clock at night, everyone was eager to make a start. The camera grab was lowered down—just to see what underwater conditions were like. On the monitor in the ship's wheelhouse they could see the sea bed without the grab actually resting on it, and they could see some wreckage as well. The magic eye had achieved its first success—and with the first grabful they filled three sacks with pieces of the smashed Victor. (Plate 13*a*.)

In nine hours next day, using the observation chamber and large grab, *Twyford* recovered 13 grabsful of wreckage. There were two torn tyres from the huge multi-wheeled undercarriage, the braking parachute with the tail swivel still attached, and twisted pieces of metal with small holes from which the rivets had been torn out piecemeal. Most of the wreckage looked as though the plane had been put through a giant mincer. Picked at random from the pile on deck, 92 pieces had gone into one sack. Later, from the residue of mud, sand and shells—a huge mud pie which was carefully raked through before being hosed over the side—over 200 pieces were put into an ordinary bucket.

The following Sunday the *Twyford* went in with her second

consignment, 30 cwt. of Victor bomber. Apart from the parachute, the heaviest piece—a mangled section of one of the
engines—weighed less than half a hundredweight. The longest
piece measured four and a half feet.

Strong, small mesh nets were made up ashore into specially
designed trawls, and on April 27th the *Twyford* took them out
and passed them over to the trawlers. They were an immediate
success. The very first haul brought up 565 pieces and that same
evening—with a new sickle moon above the setting sun, a
cloudless sky soon to be filled with myriads of twinkling stars,
and a barely ruffled sea—the trawlers, one by one, went alongside the *Twyford* to transfer their 'catches'. Their decks could
take no more. Then, as the last trawler left and as if in honour
of their success, they were all entertained by a late night fire-
works display—the *aurora borealis*.

It started at exactly 11 o'clock with a faint arc of light above
the northern horizon. The light, at first, was like a wide, diffused
whitish rainbow which then changed into dozens of waving
and flickering 'searchlights', as though a whole battery of them
was operating from away down below the rim of the sea. Then
came spurts of red, green and orange as from a gigantic fire of
gassy coal and then, within seconds, back into 'searchlights'
again. At ten minutes past midnight they went down like lights
in a cinema fading at the end of an interval, and then—out.
One could almost hear the click of an imaginary switch.

Next morning the trawlers called on the *Twyford* again and
delivered the proceeds of their night's 'fishing', and when the
Twyford went into Milford Haven that evening her fore deck
looked rather like No. 1 Platform at King's Cross station after
the arrival of the night mail. Piled up on the hatch and spilling
over on to the fore deck were 24 large canvas bags crammed
full of aircraft wreckage and 23 separate pieces, each too long
or too wide or too jagged to be put into a bag, and even a fish-
basket full. Two and a quarter tons, in all, of Victor bomber.

By April 20th an estimated one fifth of the aircraft, in weight,
was back at Farnborough, but although the total number of
pieces recovered was soaring steadily, the weight—the real
criterion of success—was not keeping pace. In early May three
more trawlers were added to the search force and the *Twyford*

was being kept out of the moor, and given other jobs, for longer and longer periods in order to let the trawlers in.

Saturday May 28th was a record day—5,014 pieces—in a record week in which a total of 16,000 pieces were recovered by the ten ships constituting the search force at that time. June 16th created a new day record of 7,271 pieces, only to be broken on the following day with 9,298, and broken yet again the next day with a total of over 13,200 pieces of wreckage. But those 13,200 pieces weighed less than eight hundredweight—an average of a fraction over one ounce per piece. There must have been a very fine cutter on that giant mincer.

Now, obviously, it was a job for trawlers alone, and when the *Twyford* slipped from the moorings on Monday, June 20th she did so for the last time. She was to be given other, though less glorious, jobs to do but that afternoon, in her last hour of grabbing, the whales gave her a sort of going-away party. There was a whole school of them within half a mile of the ship, blowing and lifting their huge tails right out of the water as they went down, and—strangest sight of all—waving their long slender flippers at the men watching them—or so it seemed. They were humpback whales, which attain a length of 40 feet when fully grown with flippers nearly a third of the length of their bodies, and have the curious habit of rolling over on their sides when about to dive and waving the uppermost flipper in the air. It was a most unexpected but rather 'human' gesture— as though they were waving goodbye to everybody.

In the last week in June two more trawlers were engaged and a month later, with a total of 16 trawlers working 18 hours a day, just over half of the Victor had been recovered. The *Twyford*'s own contribution, by grabbing, had been between three and a half and four tons.

On July 26th the BBC announced in the 6 o'clock news that the search for the Victor bomber had already cost £1,500,000 and that the total number of pieces recovered exceeded 150,000. But there was still nearly half of the aircraft on the bottom and what they needed now were 'brooms' (like the gremlins had) and not a 'pick and shovel' such as the *Twyford* had been using. Her useful rôle was at an end and she was given her discharge—albeit an honourable one—on Wednesday

August 3rd. For the last few weeks she had been maid of all work and collector of wreckage, but now it was time for her to go.

The previous evening she had bid the trawlers farewell and good 'fishing' as they came alongside in turn and delivered the proceeds of three days trawling. The *Twyford* spent the night at anchor and early next morning went into Milford Haven with her last consignment of aircraft wreckage—25,673 pieces of Victor in 11 sacks. Then she steamed out of Milford Haven and turned south. Thirty miles to the westward, the trawlers she had left to finish the job were hard at work, taking full advantage of a brief spell of summer weather, and those on board the *Twyford* wondered when, and by whose lucky hand, the piece which was to provide the final answer would be picked out of a trawl. The evening before, it had been announced that the Air Ministry had cancelled part of their order for Victor Mark 2 bombers, and they thought 'have they also been wondering, not only when and by whose hand—but IF'. Then, as they steamed away for the last time and the Pembrokeshire coast became a smudge on the horizon astern, it might have been the French Riviera they were leaving behind, so blue and smooth was the sea—and so blue the sky.

On November 19th, 1960, what was probably the greatest search operation of its kind ever undertaken was brought to a close, and two days later an official press release stated that RAE Farnborough was reasonably satisfied that they knew the cause of the accident, but that this would not have been possible without the evidence obtained from the wreckage. Perhaps the piece which provided the final answer had indeed been picked out of a trawl.

During the $13\frac{1}{2}$ months from September 1st, 1959 when the operation started, a total of 40 ships and 1,450 men had taken part in the search at sea. Trawlers had shot and hauled their nets a total of 13,236 times, of which 1,367 had been before the discovery of the first piece of wreckage. As in the case of the Comet six years earlier, about 70 per cent of the aircraft had been salvaged and taken by air to Farnborough—but this 70 per cent was in 532,618 pieces.

Jig, Saw and Puzzle had been aptly named.

CHAPTER TWELVE

THE *THRESHER*

The ultimate in streamlining, a submarine has, nevertheless, an ugly purpose. Made for killing from under the water, its life in war can be nothing more than a gamble. In peace it can perish only by its own failures or mistakes—by failure of the human element inside or by the mistakes of its designers. By the very nature of its being it is a sinister, beastly and dangerous thing.

Like a gigantic killer shark to be, the United States nuclear-powered submarine *Thresher* began to take shape in 1958. Her 'backbone' was laid down on May 28th of that year but it was nearly two years later, on July 9th, 1960, that she first took to the water. Another nine months passed before she was ready for sea.

On April 30th, 1961, with 129 men on board, the submarine slid out of Portsmouth in New Hampshire and headed sea-wards for her initial trials. On the surface the huge hull, showing little except the top of her back and sleek conning tower, displaced over 3,500 tons of water. She was over 278 feet long and 31 feet from side to side of her almost circular fish-shaped hull and had cost 45,000,000 dollars.

Then followed a long period of exercises and tests. Down south to the Bahamas, then back north to home waters for torpedo tube acceptance trials. South again for more trials and more exercises.

On April 9th, 1963, after a long overhaul which had begun on July 16th in the previous year, the *Thresher* was again ready for sea. For the second time she left the New Hampshire naval yard where she was built and headed east, escorted by the submarine rescue ship *Skylark*. *Thresher* then made an initial shallow-water test dive. All was well and at 3 p.m. she dived again and once more headed east. Her next assignment was a rendezvous with *Skylark* about 200 miles east of Cape Cod for deep dive tests just off the continental shelf.

Both ships steamed through the long dark night, the one above and the other, silently, below. At 6.35 the following morning they kept their appointment. *Thresher* came up to periscope depth about 10 miles from the *Skylark* and at 7.47 a.m. informed her escort that she was beginning her deep test dive, probably—although she did not say so—to between 800 and 1,000 feet. The exact depth of that test had to be a closely guarded secret, but the ocean floor beneath the spot where her periscope saw, on that spring morning, the light of day for the the very last time, was 8,400 feet down.

She was never to see war, and she had seen precious little of the peace. She had dived for the last time.

At 7.53 a.m. she reported by under-water telephone that she was at 400 feet and at 8.27 that she was proceeding to test depth. Forty-five minutes later, at 9.12 a.m., the two vessels made a routine check with each other.

Up above the *Thresher*, underneath the morning sky, it was peacefully calm. Only a slight swell brought the almost un-ruffled sea to life, and the gentle breeze and equally gentle undulating movement of the water must have lulled all those who, at that time and place, had gone down to the sea in ships, into a sense of tranquillity as they went about their duties.

The routine check at 9.12 on that morning of April 10th, 1963 was the last clear communication ever to be made with *Thresher*. About one minute later a voice came up over the under-water telephone and said something about 'minor difficulties', that the submarine had a 'positive up angle' and that they were 'attempting to blow'. Those aboard the *Skylark* then heard the rushing sound of compressed air being released, sounds which were associated with the normal blowing of

water from a submarine's ballast tanks which enables her to
surface. Then, a few minutes later, fragments of a garbled
message in which the only identifiable words were 'test' and
'depth'. Then silence.

Skylark fixed her position at that moment as 41 degrees 45
minutes North, 64 degrees 59 minutes West and that of the
Thresher at the last transmission as 41 degrees 44 minutes North,
64 degrees 57 minutes West, less than two miles away. They
were some 220 miles east of Cape Cod and in 8,400 feet of water.

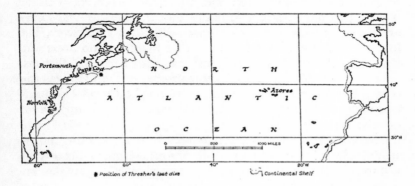

* Position of Thresher's last dive   Continental Shelf

Using her sonar, radio and under-water telephone, *Skylark*
made repeated but unsuccessful attempts to resume contact
with the submarine. Then, at 10.40 a.m., she began dropping
explosive signals which, if heard, would indicate to *Thresher*
that she should surface without delay. They also went un-
answered and at 11.04, Eastern Standard Time, *Skylark*
notified her base that she had been unable to communicate
with *Thresher* since 09.17 EST.

Although it was just possible that the submarine had been
unable to reply to her escort's signals because of a communica-
tions failure, it was also possible that her silence had resulted
from something far more disastrous. The situation, obviously,
demanded the organization of an immediate search.

By 8 o'clock that evening it had been decided at the headquarters of Naval Operations at the Pentagon that the *Thresher*
must be presumed lost and that the dreaded news must be
imparted to the next of kin of all those on board.

Already, other naval ships had arrived to assist *Skylark*, and during the night a further five ships—two destroyers, two other submarines and a frigate—joined the search. Six more ships and a fleet tanker arrived before noon on the 11th when the search force came under the command of Rear Admiral Ramage, Deputy Commander of the Atlantic Submarine Force, on board the U.S. destroyer *Blandy*. In the afternoon, two naval aircraft carrying press representatives flew over the search area and by the evening of the same day the whole world knew of the disaster. The Secretary of the Navy issued from Washington an official notice that the *Thresher* was lost— and that there was absolutely no possibility of any survivors. The bereaved families also knew, then, that there was no hope and that 187 children had suddenly and tragically become fatherless.

One of the ships which joined the force on the 11th was the oceanographic research ship *Atlantis II*. She had special bottom-sounding equipment and was also able to pick up actual samples from the sea bed.

Gale warnings for the area had been issued that same morning and already the wind and a rising sea had joined forces with a lowering temperature and blustery showers to make an already unpleasant job even more unpleasant.

While ships and submarines began methodically searching the hundred square miles around the position of the *Thresher*'s last dive, and recovered various objects which may, or may not, have come from the entombed submarine—two rubber gloves, pieces of cork and plastic, a tube of cook's flavouring—the *Atlantis* commenced mapping the ocean floor. She was looking for any irregularity which might be the wrecked *Thresher*. Eight more research and survey ships joined in.

In the ten days up to April 22nd, a dozen contacts were made. Six of them warranted further investigation. Underwater cameras mounted with powerful lights and sounding equipment were lowered to within 15 to 30 feet of the sea bed, but the task of photographing an object on the ocean floor with the camera swinging about on the end of a mile and a half of control cable, suspended from a ship above which is, itself, being tossed about on a turbulent sea, was not without difficulty.

THE 'THRESHER'

To make the problem of identifying the hull of the *Thresher* an easier one, plans were made to sink an old submarine in the search area so that the ships could 'follow her down' to the sea bed with their sonar devices and so have a fairly accurate picture of what the wrecked *Thresher* would look like lying on the bottom. But by the middle of May, and before this plan could be put into operation, photographs of the ocean floor in the vicinity of where *Thresher* had gone down had shown several small metallic objects which might have come from the lost submarine, though they could not be positively identified as such. Then, on May 27th, another of the research ships, the *Conrad*, brought up in her dredge 19 small packages of rubber washers, used as sealing rings in various types of submarine hydraulic machinery. Each of the packets bore stock numbers. The numbers were traced and six of them were found to correspond with those supplied to *Thresher*.

Conrad's under-water cameras took more photographs around the position. Of the 500 sequences taken on one roll of film, eight showed what were thought to be portions of the lost submarine. One was a part of the hull, another was thought to be the *Thresher*'s 'sail' or conning tower, and another a diving plane. Spurred on by these momentous discoveries, the famous 51-ton bathyscaph *Trieste* which the U.S. government had purchased from Professor Auguste Piccard in 1958, was prepared at Boston to be towed out to the search area and dive on the spot where the *Conrad* had photographed the objects.

On May 31st, the photographs were flown to Washington for detailed examination by experts—and then time went back. They were definitely not *Thresher* wreckage. They might not be pictures of submarine wreckage at all. In fact it was thought that the camera had, possibly, been looking at bits of its own anchor and lead weight—and a close-up of the lead weight could be mistaken for the *Thresher*'s sail. The official news release on Saturday, June 1st, merely said that 'although some objects in the picture remain unidentified, none could be identified as being any part of the *Thresher*'. The rubber washers remained the only positive clues to the lost submarine's whereabouts, and they might have been carried miles away from where the *Thresher* now lay. In the face of this setback it was decided

161

that the *Trieste* would remain in Boston until the exact location of the sunken *Thresher* was established.

Another research ship, the *Gilliss*, joined the search force on Monday, June 3rd. Her immediate rôle was to take bottom photographs with her closed circuit television camera.

Another two weeks of searching and then, in the middle of June, the *Conrad* again produced photographs of interesting objects. They included an air bottle, a piece of broken piping and a metal plate about nine feet long and eight feet wide. Having already been the victim of some wishful thinking, all that the Navy Photographic Interpretation Center would say was that the materials were of the type used in naval ship construction. They were understandably wary of pronouncing a definite affirmative but they were, obviously, hopeful enough; preparations went ahead for the *Trieste* to dive on the new position, and the sinking of the old submarine was cancelled.

The *Trieste* arrived in the search area on June 23rd and on the following morning, at 10.35, started on her 8,400-foot journey to the floor of the ocean. An hour later she began searching. Her eyes were those of the observers in her 7-foot diameter observation gondola on the bottom of her hull and four external cameras. Her ears—a sonar with a 400-yard range. Her arms were combined in a remote-controlled external claw. She covered about two square miles of ocean floor—looking, turning and searching—from about 40 feet off the bottom. She surfaced just before 4 p.m., having seen nothing of any significance. On the 26th she spent another four hours on the bottom, and picked up sonar echoes from an object estimated to be about 60 feet long. It had given a metallic 'return' but they had lost it after two minutes contact.

Next day she went down again to look for her 60-foot object. She did not find it, but she did see a yellow rubber shoe cover of the type used aboard nuclear submarines. It actually bore the Attack Nuclear Submarine identifying letters 'SSN' and a figure which was one of the digits in the *Thresher*'s hull number. She also saw a mass of paper and other lightweight wreckage believed to have come from the *Thresher*.

So it went on. On a subsequent dive, the *Trieste* followed a trail of such débris across the bottom. At the end of it were two craters. Had the doomed submarine plunged down, end on, only to bury itself deep in the bottom ooze? All kinds of explanations were suggested but nothing was confirmed. *Trieste* made five dives in all and photographed a number of objects and pieces of wreckage and then, on July 1st, set off on her four-day tow back to Boston for overhaul and refit. (Plate 13*b*.)

Most of the supporting force set off likewise into port, leaving one research ship to continue searching with under-water cameras and sonar. But it was not the end. Although there was by then, no doubt about the fate of the *Thresher*, they were determined to make every effort to locate her hull. The official news release, on June 20th, of the Court of Inquiry findings said that "the Navy believes it most likely that a piping system failure had occurred in one of *Thresher*'s salt water systems, probably in the engine room. The enormous pressure of sea water surrounding the submarine subjected her interior to a violent spray of water and progressive flooding. In all probability water affected electrical circuits and caused loss of power. *Thresher* slowed and began to sink. Within moments she had exceeded her collapse depth and totally flooded. She came to rest on the ocean floor, 8,400 feet beneath the surface."

"She came to rest . . .". There could be no more fitting epitaph, but the search for her remains went on.

In a press release issued by the Department of Defense on August 2nd it was stated: "The Navy will send the deep-diving bathyscaph *Trieste* to sea in mid-August for a new series of dives in search of the sunken nuclear submarine *Thresher*." In her five previous dives she had discovered "a considerable amount of débris" but had failed to locate the hull of the submarine.

By the time the *Trieste* was back for the renewed hunt, nearly two square miles of the ocean floor in the search area had been, quite literally, signposted. An oceanographic tug had planted over 1,440 plastic 'flowers' in the under-water garden where the *Thresher* had laid herself down for her everlasting sleep. There were 11 rows—nearly 8,000 feet long and 750 feet apart—of coloured discs which were anchored by weighted cords. The *Trieste* could search the lanes, one by one, and establish her position instantly just by looking at the nearest signpost. There was no need for traffic lights—there was only one automobile. Of

course, it did not go quite like that. It was, after all, nearly one
and a half miles down and she was not an automobile on a road
nor was there daylight where she was going. Others things, too.
intervened. *Trieste*'s first dive was planned for Monday, August
19th but bad weather, which had put one of the navigation
buoys out of position, and faults in equipment conspired to
delay the descent for four days. Even then, fog prevented the
start of the dive until late in the day when she spent only just
over an hour on the bottom. Then a warning that hurricane
'Beulah' might be moving their way sent most of the force
northwards—one of the ships with *Trieste* in tow. But 'Beulah'
decided not to trouble them after all and they turned back as
soon as it was certain that she had veered away.

By September 1st the *Trieste* had made another four descents
—five dives in all in the second phase of the search operations.
Nothing was made known at that time of what, if anything, she
had seen or found but it really was the end. On the 5th, the
Secretary of the Navy authorized the Department of Defense to
release a statement which ran:

> "The location of structural parts of the *Thresher* on the
> ocean floor having been confirmed by the bathyscaph *Trieste*
> during her latest series of successful dives, I have today
> directed that the associated operational aspects of the
> search for the nuclear submarine *Thresher* be terminated.
>
> "The latest series of five dives by the *Trieste* have been
> tremendously successful. In her third dive, on August 24,
> 1963, the bathyscaph took a number of extremely valuable
> photographs and made a unique recovery from the ocean
> floor. The item recovered was a length of copper piping and a
> fitting with markings which definitely established that it
> came from the *Thresher*. The piping was picked up by a
> mechanical arm operated from inside the *Trieste*'s gondola
> in the first successful test of this device.
>
> "More than three dozen ships and thousands of men have
> been engaged for nearly five months in detailed probings of
> the ocean floor where the *Thresher* lies in 8,400 feet of water.
> These efforts, combined with the evidence gathered by
> *Trieste* during the latest series of dives, have produced con-

clusive information that we know the general area where the
Thresher lies. We are equally sure that she poses no hazard,
even to marine life. . . ."

That was part of the statement read at the press conference,
and the 'length of copper piping and a fitting' was there on a
table for all to see. The piece of piping was 57 inches long. The
fitting was a rusty bracket. The piping and bracket together
weighed about 10 pounds. Just 10 of the *Thresher*'s original
8,500,000 pounds of killer submarine was all that had been
brought back. The rest with the 129 men on board lay undisturbed for ever in her watery tomb nearly one and a half miles
down.

CHAPTER THIRTEEN

THE *SCORPION*

Following the tragedy of the *Thresher*, the maximum permitted depth at which Attack Nuclear Submarines could operate was limited and a Submarine Safety Improvement programme, to be known as 'SubSafe', was developed.

The *Trieste* was towed back to Boston and shipped to the Naval Electronics Laboratory at San Diego in California, her home base. There she was to undergo complete overhaul, including installation of new hull and repositioning of her observation gondola. She was, in fact, to be changed so much that it was as *Trieste II* that she eventualy returned to Boston in April 1964 to continue with oceanographic research around *Thresher*'s last resting place. (Plate 14*a*.)

Meanwhile, Attack Nuclear Submarines went on exercising and diving. Memories of the *Thresher*'s loss, except perhaps for those who had been so abruptly robbed of husbands, sons or fathers, became dimmed as time went by. It had been, maybe, some chance-in-a-million failure or a once-in-a-lifetime human error. Years passed, and submarines departed, dived, glided through the waters of the oceans and arrived, according to schedule. Missions were planned, executed and completed, according to plan. All seemed well again.

Five years had passed since that tragic April day in 1963, when another Attack Nuclear Submarine, the *Scorpion* with a crew of 99 men, was homeward bound across the Atlantic from

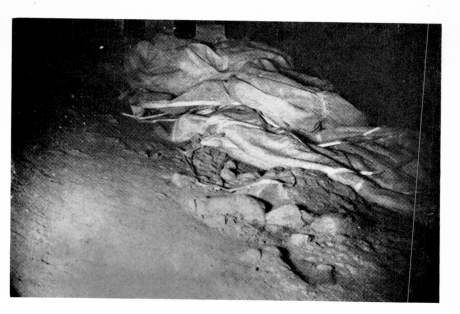

Plate 15a, Bomb shrouded in parachute
photographed by CURV

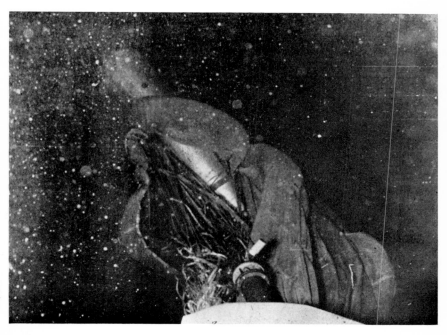

Plate 15b, Bomb with parachute cut away

Plate 16*a*, Cable-controlled Underwater
Research Vehicle, CURV

Plate 16*b*, Nuclear weapon on board
USS *Petrel*, with CURV in background

European waters. Although the *Scorpion*'s last major overhaul, ending in May 1964, had been completed before all the recommendations of SubSafe could be incorporated some of the measures had already been passed to shipyards. She was also subjected to a detailed examination when she drydocked in the summer of 1967 and only seven minor faults were reported during her subsequent trials in October of that year.

It was now 1968 and she was scheduled to arrive in Norfolk, Virginia at 1 p.m. on May 27th. It had been a long lonely journey but all was well. On the evening of the 21st, in the vicinity of the Azores, she had made a signal to this effect and was known to be operating normally.

This was, too, a normal routine passage—not deep diving trials as was the case with *Thresher*. There was, too, no escorting ship near at hand to say 'this is where we saw her last' but no great concern was felt until *Scorpion* failed to arrive, or make any further signal, by early afternoon on May 27th.

It is about 2,300 miles from the Azores to Norfolk in Virginia, and the submarine's route would have taken her through waters where the ocean floor drops away to over 21,004 feet deep—nearly four nautical miles. The *Thresher*'s possible graveyard had been a mere few square miles. If the *Scorpion* was lost, she might be anywhere in those 2,300 miles of ocean bed.

The Attack Nuclear Submarine USS *Scorpion* was declared 'overdue in Norfolk, Virginia since 1 p.m. on May 27th', and by the following morning submarines and destroyers were scouring the western end of the *Scorpion*'s intended track, from Norfolk eastwards to the 300-foot contour. By the 29th, more than 30 aircraft, flying in from the Azores, Bermuda and Norfolk bases, were searching along the entire route, right from the Azores to the Virginian coast. It was a gigantic search area. They covered the track and 25 miles either side of it, a total expanse of some 115,000 square miles of ocean. And while they searched from the air, over 50 ships were engaged in surface operations.

On the 23rd, four days before the scheduled arrival of the *Scorpion* and two days after her last radio check, a ship had reported sighting an oil slick at the eastern end of the 'submarine transit lane' which extended between 550 and 600 miles east-

ward from the coast at Norfolk. At the time, no great importance seems to have been attached to this report. In any case
it was far to the westward of the submarine's expected position
on the 23rd, but now that she was overdue, aircraft were
despatched immediately to plot the oil slick but failed to find
it. On the 29th, four naval ships diverted from their original
missions arrived in the area to carry out a detailed search.

The oil slick was not found, but between 60 and 80 miles to
the north of where it had been sighted originally, one of the
crew of the USS *Hyades* reported seeing an orange-coloured
cylindrical shape floating on the water. The time was 6.15 a.m.
The date was May 28th. The crew man said a line was attached
to the object but an aircraft which was overhead at the time
failed to locate it. No one else on the ship saw it, either, and
on the following day, the 29th, the Director of Naval Operations announced at a news briefing that it had been 'identified
by its size and shape as not being associated with the
submarine'.

Ships and aircraft continued their search for the oil slick. It
had gone—or, perhaps, it had never existed. An unruffled
patch of water glinting in the sun and viewed from a ship's
deck can look very much like an oil slick and many a piece of
harmless floating débris can be mistaken for an 'orange-
coloured cylindrical object' and then afterwards, when a submarine is reported missing, wishful thinking does the rest.

So the search went on—at first in 35-knot winds, a high sea,
and in conditions of low cloud and poor visibility, at any rate in
the western part of the area. It was not exactly ideal weather
for spotting anything floating on the sea, even the *Scorpion*
herself, for at that time no one knew whether she was disabled
and still floating—or lying on the bottom, flooded and wrecked,
somewhere in that 50-mile wide lane of ocean floor, 2,300 miles
long. Even though, eventually, it was possible to eliminate three-
quarters of that enormous area, what was left would be equal
to the entire expanse of the English Channel, from Ushant and
Land's End to the Straits of Dover. At another news briefing
on the afternoon of the 29th it was stated: "the Navy does not
know the location of the *Scorpion*. She is still listed simply as
overdue".

While two submarines and a submarine rescue vessel continued to concentrate on the shallower water between the coast at Norfolk and the edge of the continental shelf, about 65 miles out—where the sea floor falls away steeply from the 600 foot level right down to over 6,000 feet within a few miles—the rest of the searching ships, aircraft and submarines, did their utmost to cover the remainder of that long, long road across the Atlantic.

In the western part of the search area 11 ships were spread out across that wide lane of seaway. Three covered the centre of the lane, the most likely path of the homeward-bound *Scorpion*, three more the northern fringe and three more to the southward, but slightly astern of the central three. Behind those nine, as a kind of longstop, two more ships followed.

Between them they had to cover 50 miles of sea and so, allowing for marginal overlaps, each vessel would have been responsible for about two and a half miles of ocean surface on either side. From high look-outs and in reasonable weather, and with radar constantly scanning the ocean surface, nothing of any size which was still floating could have passed unnoticed.

The weather had already improved by the 30th and the chances of missing anything of importance consequently diminished. Still nothing was seen. The ships steamed on, like a cordon of policemen at arm's length apart, searching the countryside for a body.

One particular place, however, came in for special attention. About 420 miles from the Azores and 60 miles southward of the intended track of the submarine, there is a shallow patch. Shallow, that is, by comparison with surrounding depths, but still well over 300 feet. Another nuclear submarine, the *Gato*, was despatched to make a detailed under-water sonar search in the vicinity of that submerged mountain peak. Suppose the *Scorpion* had been cruising just below that depth, and had gone off course. After all, she had already come quite a long way and she could have gone to the southward for some reason. The *Gato* was due to arrive in the area on the 31st.

The main force searched on. Additional units followed between 100 and 150 miles astern, constituting a second line of searchers.

Submarines carry a buoy which can be released from a submerged vessel and which, on reaching the surface, begins transmitting a distress signal. None had been heard by any ship or aircraft. Even after the transmitter had stopped operating, the buoy would remain afloat. Nothing had been seen.

The *Scorpion* could have been lying on the bottom, disabled but intact and without power or means of communication, in relatively shallow water. If her oxygen and life-sustaining equipment were undamaged her crew could remain alive for months. But in such relatively shallow water—anywhere, for instance, on the continental shelf—some if not all of her crew could have escaped. At that time it was already considered practicable for men to escape from a submarine as deep as 600 feet by individual ascent through the escape hatch. This hatch is a small separate compartment with access from inside the submarine and exit above into the sea. After the man has entered and closed the bottom hatch from inside, escape is made possible by forcing air into the compartment until the pressure inside equals that of the water outside. The exit hatch can then be opened and the man rises buoyantly to the surface, exhaling the high pressure air as he rises.

This method of escape was explained at a news briefing by the Director of the Navy's Deep Submergence Project and held at the Pentagon on May 29th, when it was also stated that "our submarines are equipped to permit the crew to be locked-out in this manner". At the same briefing the Navy Medical Corps Assistant for Medical Effects said that he himself had come up from a depth of 320 feet by this method, wearing no special gear other than an inflatable life-jacket. He said "we took approximately 25 seconds to pressurize the escape compartment, about 12 more seconds checking our gear, and stepped out of the submarine and took 57 seconds to reach the surface." It was then that he stated that he considered that this method was practicable down to 600 feet but, he went on, "beyond that depth it does not seem feasible to have individual escape because of the need for extremely rapid pressurization in order to get the man out and on his way so that he has not absorbed enough inert gas to develop the bends, and also because of the fact that narcosis, the rapture of the deeps, attacks a man very rapidly at depths like this and much worse as you go deeper".

Night and day the search continued. Nothing was found—no submarine, no survivors, and no wreckage. Nothing to indicate where the *Scorpion* was, or what had happened to her, had been discovered by any of the searching ships and aircraft. Then, on June 5th, this statement was issued by the Chief of Naval Operations to the press:

"It is my sad duty to declare that the United States Ship *Scorpion* and her crew of 99 men are presumed lost, though our search efforts will continue. *Scorpion* has been overdue since 1 p.m. on May 27th, the date she was scheduled to arrive in her home port of Norfolk, Virginia, and has not been heard of since the evening of May 21st, at which time she was operating normally while returning home.

"Now, because of the lack of any evidence of *Scorpion*'s presence on the surface or in waters which would permit rescue, we must conclude that she was lost in the depths of the Atlantic. This conclusion is further based on the fact that we have had no signals in the form of sonar or radio transmissions, flares or messenger buoys, nor have we observed any débris specifically identifiable with *Scorpion*. These facts compel us to conclude that she is not in a location where recovery of the crew could be effected or salvage conducted."

The great search did continue, throughout the whole summer of that year, 1968. One of the additional ships called in was the U.S. Navy's oceanographic research ship *Mizar*, the same *Mizar* which had photographed wreckage of the *Thresher* in 1963. With her remote-control under-water cameras she searched the ocean floor—and success came at last.

On October 29th, about 400 miles south-west of the Azores, she found the *Scorpion*'s hull, resting on the bottom nearly 2 miles down. Disaster had come to her a long, long way from home. (Plate 14*b*.)

The news was released to the world two days later. In an announcement to the press on October 31st the Chief of Naval Operations stated: "Objects identified as portions of the hull of the submarine USS *Scorpion* have been located about 400 miles south-west of the Azores in more than 10,000 feet of water. The Navy received the information from *Mizar*, a U.S. Navy oceanographic ship, on the evening of October 30th. This culminates the most extensive sea search ever conducted, extending over a period of five months and involving more than 40 ships, over 6,000 men and numerous aircraft. *Mizar* reports that the submarine's location has been confirmed by means of remotely controlled underwater photography."

As a direct result of *Mizar*'s remarkable discovery the Court of Inquiry, originally opened on June 5th and then adjourned after sitting for seven weeks, was re-convened, and *Mizar* stayed on to try and photograph more of the *Scorpion*'s hull and thereby produce further evidence which would enable the Court to establish the cause of the disaster.

The *Mizar* found more, and took thousands of photographs but still the mystery remained unsolved. More than three months after *Mizar*'s initial discovery, and on the last day of January 1969, the Navy announced the findings of the second phase of the Court of Inquiry: "The certain cause of the loss of the *Scorpion* cannot be ascertained from any evidence now available. Identifiable débris does not lead to a determination of the cause for the loss of the *Scorpion*."

Although it was then more than eight months since the submarine had disappeared, and although portions of the hull had been found and photographed, it was not the end. In still greater efforts to unravel the enigma, the *Trieste*—now *Trieste II*—was called in and began a new phase of the operation early in 1969. In the words of the official news release which announced this intention the Navy said "*Trieste* can carry one observer in addition to its two-man crew. Various technical experts thus will be able to conduct on the spot visual inspections of *Scorpion*'s hull through the use of spotlights. The bathyscaph has been modified to improve its capabilities for controlled mobility. *Trieste* crewmen will be able to photograph the submarine's wreckage from different angles than were possible with the *Mizar*'s towed under-water cameras. Additionally, *Trieste* has a limited capability to retrieve small objects from the ocean floor."

Although the precise cause of the loss of the *Scorpion* remained a complete mystery, the Court of Inquiry was, from the examination of the 232 numbered exhibits and 1,334 pages of evidence from 90 witnesses, 'able to eliminate two possible causes based on available facts. It was able to conclude that the *Scorpion* did not hit a seamount, since there is none in the area where the submarine went to the bottom. After hearing the expert testimony of qualified witnesses, the Court also dismissed the nuclear reactor plant as a possible cause of the loss.'

The Court also 'found no evidence that collision with another submarine or ship caused *Scorpion*'s loss. No U.S. ships or submarines reported such a collision nor have those of any other nation. Additionally, no wreckage other than *Scorpion*'s has appeared in the thousands of photographs taken by *Mizar*.'

If not the machine what, then, of the men?

In the final relevant extract from the findings, the news release of January 31st gave the answer. The Court had stated that 'the evidence does not establish that the loss of the *Scorpion* and deaths of those embarked were caused by the intent, fault, negligence or inefficiency of any person or persons in the naval service or connected therewith'.

Like the men of the *Thresher* before them, the ninety-nine knew, all too grimly, the other and more infinite meaning of 'those who go down to the sea in ships'. Would it have been easier for them had they known, also, that their fellow men had judged that it was by a hand other than their own?

CHAPTER FOURTEEN

PALOMARES

Sometime before dawn on January 16th, 1966, a giant B-52G jet bomber of the United States Air Force took off from its base in North Carolina and headed east. It was to fly first over Spain, then eastwards over the Mediterranean and on to the western borders of the Soviet Union. There, on its assigned air-borne alert station, it would remain before turning west and heading back for home. That was the programme—a dull, monotonous routine flight for Strategic Air Command which was destined, tragically, never to be completed.

Six hours after leaving home on the outward flight, the B-52, with its companion bomber, kept a rendezvous with two KC-135 refuelling tankers over Spain, filled its emptying tanks and then, flying high at about 600 miles an hour, continued eastwards. On board was a crew of seven and four 5,000-pound plutonium-uranium-235 hydrogen bombs, two in each bomb bay.

On ordinary routine flights there would have been a crew of only six but this was an airborne alert mission—a mission involving a non-stop flight which took them twice across the Atlantic and twice the length of the Mediterranean, with an all-night patrol sandwiched in between the outward and home-ward journeys. An extra pilot was an operational necessity.

Besides, the bombs were not harmless dummies. The B-52 was fully prepared for serious business—if it should ever come to that. If it ever should, one of the crew—an electronic warfare officer—would have a rather frightening and gruesome task. If that dreaded order for nuclear attack was received, he would be the one to complete the complicated and secret procedure which would turn those four products of man's satanic ingenuity into the most devastating weapons ever known. These nuclear bombs, carried by all B-52s on such missions, were, paradoxically as it may seem, harmless enough. They were what is known as 'unarmed'; that is, they were capable of nuclear reaction only when certain secret things were done to them.

By the time the B-52 reached its patrol area, somewhere to the westward of the Turkish-Soviet boundary, it was already dark. At about 50,000 feet, its long night of vigil began without incident, then continued monotonously and uneventfully until, as the sky lightened over Russia to the east, the aircraft turned for home. It had been duly relieved. Another loaded B-52 had taken over.

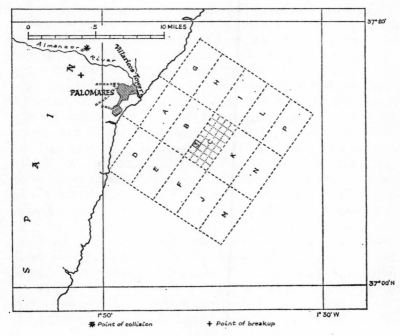

Its route home took it back over south-east Spain, to another rendezvous with a refuelling tanker for, although these giant bombers have a fuel range of 7,500 miles, alert missions so far from home would not have been feasible without a double refuelling. At about the same time as the rising sun came up over the horizon astern of the B-52, and more than 2,000 miles away to the westward, ahead of the bomber, the refuelling tankers were preparing to leave their base at Moron near Seville. Each of the two swept-wing KC-135s was loading up with more than 110 tons of jet kerosene for which the two B-52s, each with eight turbo-jet engines, would be eagerly waiting in a few hours time. After twice flying the whole length of the Mediterranean from end to end and flying round in circles for the whole of one night, they would be in dire need of their breakfast time 'drink' to get them back home. It was about nine o'clock, local time, on January 17th, when the loaded tankers took off into the clear blue sky of that fateful January morning. Refuelling the returning B-52s was a daily task for the Spanish-based KC-135 tankers, and for others at other places. In fact, at that time, one SAC bomber, somewhere, was being refuelled in the air, on an average, every six minutes of the day.

Bomber and tanker were due to meet at the seaward end of the 70-mile long refuelling track, over 30,000 feet above the Almanzora River, known as the Saddle Rock Refuelling Area. Soon after ten o'clock the KC-135 entered the track approach twenty-one miles ahead of the B-52 in preparation for the hook up. Although it is done so frequently, refuelling in the air calls for a high degree of skill and aerial manœuvring. The aircraft taking the fuel comes up behind the tanker and slightly below it. The tanker lowers its fuelling boom, the other aircraft gradually closes up, the connection is made and the transfer of fuel takes place while both aircraft are flying at, in this case, 275 miles an hour.

On this January morning over south-east Spain, the B-52 and the KC-135 tanker were about to hook up. They were about half a mile apart, with the bomber 150 feet below and astern of the tanker. They had been in radio contact for some minutes and everything was proceeding normally. The tanker boom operator was talking Captain Wendorf, piloting the B-52, into the intricate manœuvre for the actual hook-up, when he realized that the other aircraft was coming in too fast—and too close. He shouted a warning over the radio—but it was too late. In the B-52 Captain Wendorf also saw, but too late, that he was too near—and flying too fast. As the starboard wing of the huge 134-ton tanker cast its shadow over the B-52s cockpit, there was a gigantic shudder as the two aircraft collided, the almost 180-ton bomber inexorably entangled with the flying tank of jet fuel above it. The ensuing explosion shook the coast nearly six miles below as the fiery mass went hurtling onwards. As the B-52 started breaking up, the navigator had a job to do. He had a button to press. The explosion which resulted was a small one compared with what had happened a few seconds before, but in the forward section of the bomber—or what was left of it—the navigator and his three companions knew no more.

At twenty-two minutes past ten the other KC-135 was preparing to rendezvous with the second B-52 only a few miles away. They heard the explosion, saw the fiery ball against the blue sky where the first B-52 had been and radioed their base that she was on fire. They assumed it was only the bomber as they could not, then, see the tanker. From that moment, news of the disaster spread rapidly. Within three minutes, the Headquarters of the American Air Force near Madrid knew about it and ten minutes later—only thirteen minutes after the collision—the Pentagon in Washington was aware that a B-52 bomber carrying four nuclear weapons had crashed in south-east Spain. In much less than an hour the whole emergency organization of the United States Armed Forces, all over the world, had been put into operation.

A large part of the B-52s landing gear with one giant wheel still attached, and the rear bomb bay, came down on the northern outskirts of Palomares. The 85-foot long right wing of the bomber was found west of the village in a tomato field. Charred bodies, burning engines and flaming wreckage—aftermath of the holocaust which had come out of the skies—shattered the peace of Palomares on that sunny morning in January. Mercifully, the 115 tons of jet fuel in the tanker and nearly as much still in the B-52 had evaporated in the air five miles up after the collision, thus avoiding another and much fiercer holocaust on the ground. As it was, houses, people and animals all miraculously escaped damage or injury.

At sea, the crew of a Spanish fishing boat five miles off shore had heard the explosion, seen the blazing wreckage in the sky and several parachutes floating down—and picked up a survivor from the B-52. Two other fishing boats, despatched by the Spanish Navy's detachment at Aguilas, picked up Captain Wendorf of the B-52 and his co-pilot, unconscious, from their inflated rafts. Their parachutes had opened automatically after falling 16,500 feet from the wrecked bomber, and then floated gently down for the remaining 14,000 feet into the sea where their rafts inflated beneath them.

The survivor rescued by the first boat, the *Manuela Orts*, was Major Messinger, Staff Pilot in the B-52. He had opened his parachute after being ejected and had taken twenty minutes to come down. After taking him on board the fishing boat turned towards another floating parachute. They had seen six parachutes altogether, floating down. One was on fire and falling much faster than the rest until it disappeared over the land. Three others were far out to sea, blown by the off-shore wind, and soon vanished. The remaining two seemed to be falling directly towards the boat and came down together within a hundred yards of her. Both appeared to have something heavy suspended from them but sank before the boat could reach either of them

The fishing boat was a local one and still in sight of the shore. The captain knew where he was and instinctively noted the position on his chart. It was 37 degrees 12 minutes North, 01 degrees 41 minutes West.

Ashore, in and around Palomares, most of the falling wreckage had been seen by someone, for the shattering explosion must have been heard by everyone for miles. The first of the four bombs was found later the same day on the sloping bank of the Almanzora River, near the sea and south-east of the village. Two local civil guards had spotted it, enveloped in its parachute, only a short distance from where the B-52s tail section had fallen. It was dented but intact.

By daybreak next morning hundreds of U.S. Army and Air Force officers and men were scouring the countryside for the three bombs still missing. To find them, or at least to know where they were, was absolutely vital. Fanning out from where the wrecked tail section lay, they systematically covered an ever increasing area, marking off patches, as soon as each one was completed, with twine so as not to go over the same ground twice. Farther afield, other areas were being marked with streamers of white toilet paper for everything, at first, was improvisation—so urgent was the finding.

By ten o'clock the second bomb had been spotted by one of the helicopters about two miles west of the village. It was without its parachute—and split wide open. Less than half an hour later, and just over half a mile west of the river embankment where the two civil guards had discovered the first one, the remains of the parachute which had been seen burning by the fishing boat was found and, lying beside it, another bomb. It, too, was split wide open.

When the two bombs had hit the ground their TNT charges exploded. Tiny particles of oxidized radio-active isotopes had been scattered over Palomares. The whole area was contaminated.

Within twenty-four hours of the tragedy, three of the four hydrogen bombs had been found, but the search force, quite suddenly and unexpectedly, had another task—to determine the limits of the contaminated ground. Meanwhile the search for the fourth $2\frac{1}{4}$-ton nuclear bomb went on even more frantically. Perhaps it also, somewhere still unknown, was a radio-active menace.

At about the same time, a Spanish-speaking interrogation officer was questioning the crews of the fishing boats and he then heard from Captain Francisco Simo Orts of the *Manuela Orts* about the parachutes with 'something heavy hanging from them' which sank near his boat. On the chart he pointed to the position he had marked the previous day. The water there was over 3,000 feet deep.

Five days of intensive searching on land had ended with no trace of the missing bomb and on Saturday, January 22nd, convinced that it had probably fallen into the sea, the United States authorities ordered a full-scale sea search in addition to the land search which was to continue unabated. Ships from the

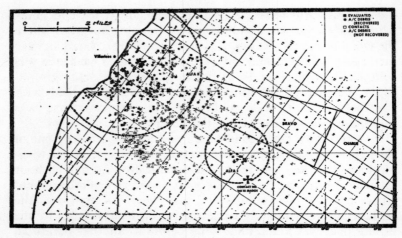

Debris pattern showing locations of contacts obtained by units
of Task Force 65.

U.S. Sixth Fleet in the Mediterranean were despatched to
the area off Palomares. Firms specializing in under-water equipment were consulted and asked to supply both material and
experts. The U.S. Navy's own specialists in under-water
television, and deep-diving research vessels were called in. The
cream of their own submarine and salvage specialist officers
were taken off whatever tasks they were engaged on and flown
to south-east Spain. So came into being 'Aircraft Salvage
Operations, Mediterranean', to be known henceforth and to go
down in history as Aircraft Salvops Med. The vessels taking
part, Task Force 65, comprised initially ten ships.

The search area, centred roughly on the position given by the
fishing boat of where the parachutes were seen to come down
and sink, was a patch of sea bed from the shore to ten miles out
to sea, stretching for twelve miles along the coast

Here they were, committed to finding an object 10 feet long
which could be almost anywhere in an area of 120 square miles
and might be anything up to 4,000 feet down. It was like looking for a pine-needle on the bottom of a swimming pool in
complete darkness. Accurate position fixing was an absolute
necessity—and Decca came to their aid. A Master Station and

two Slave Stations were specially set up ashore and any Task
Force ship equipped with the appropriate receiver could then
pinpoint her own position and, therefore, the position of
any contact on the bottom, with a maximum error of only 30
feet. The deadly 5,000-pound nuclear weapon which had to be
found was about to be hunted.

While frogmen searched the shallower waters along the
shore—diving and searching in depths down to 36 feet, and
finding more and more pieces of aircraft wreckage but no
bomb—Task Force 65 acquired its first submersible search
craft. On January 29th a fleet ocean tug arrived from Cartagena
and presented to the ships off Palomares a two-man deep-diving submarine called *Deep Jeep* which could dive to 2,000 feet
and remain below for four hours at a time, and a minesweeper
equipped with an ocean bottom scanning sonar device began
a sea bed search. In two days of being towed along above the
sea bed it found 28 'somethings'. The somethings could be
isolated rocks, pieces of wreckage—or what? Three of them
were plotted and noted as 'promising'.

Two more deep research submarines, the *Alvin* and the
Aluminaut, both then operating at American bases, were
ordered to join Task Force 65. The *Alvin*, carrying a crew of
three, was a mini-submarine only 22 feet long, 8 feet wide and
weighing 13 tons. With a submerged endurance of more than
twenty-four hours, a top speed of 4 knots, a depth range of
6,000 feet, a grappling arm, closed circuit television and a
scanning sonar she was a veritable mermaid of all work.

Her big sister, the *Aluminaut*, weighed 81 tons and although
she was 51 feet long she was a very slim sister. Her waist measurement was the same as *Alvin*'s, only 8 feet. She carried a crew of
six and could dive to 15,000 feet but, operationally, this was
limited to 6,000 feet, the same as *Alvin*'s, so that no one spot
within the search area was beyond their range. She was
equipped with every conceivable electronic aid, including
under-water television, telephone and illumination equipment,
and both she and *Alvin* were attended by a vessel, the USS *Fort
Snelling*, which had a floodable after deck for launching and
recovering the submarines.

The *Pinnacle*, the minesweeper operating the sonar device,

then took Captain Orts out to the position where he had seen the two parachutes sink—and OBSS, the Ocean Bottom Scanning Sonar, then made a contact close by at a depth of 2,000 feet.

The bottom was not exactly flat in this area. The *Pinnacle* steamed away and then returned, taking care that neither Orts nor the sonar operator knew when they were back over the spot. Again a contact was reported. Another minesweeper with a detecting device was called in and she also recorded a contact at 2,000 feet. Both of these were considered interesting but, at that time, the depth was too great for immediate identification. The place did, however, acquire a new name— High Probability Area.

The *Alvin* and *Aluminaut* arrived in the search area on February 10th but high winds and bad weather contrived together to delay the start of diving operations until the 14th.

High Probability Area was a two-mile diameter circle centred on the estimated position of the two sinking parachutes and now including the bottom contact. The *Alvin* took over the southern half of the circle and the *Aluminaut* the northern portion, while 150 divers continued to work out from the shore as far as the 350 foot contour and found more than 50 tons of aircraft wreckage—but only wreckage.

By the time the submarine search was under way, the 185 men ashore, with their tractors and radiological monitoring equipment, had completed their initial task of determining the extent of the area affected by the exploding nuclear bombs. Six hundred and forty acres of ground, comprising 854 individual plots, were found to be contaminated. By agreement with Spanish Government officials, 385 acres or more than half a square mile would have to be ploughed to a depth of ten inches, and this without obliterating the boundaries of the tiny holdings; while from the ground immediately surrounding the places where the bombs had fallen and exploded, two inches of top soil over a total area of five and a half acres had to be removed and replaced with clean top soil from elsewhere. That thin slice of two inches represented nearly 1,250 tons of earth. In the end, the quantity actually shipped away was something over 1,100 tons.

On the day *Alvin* and *Aluminaut* started searching, another submersible joined the task force and took over the job of identifying wreckage between depths of 200 and 600 feet. She was soon able to clear that area of any possibility that the bomb might be found in these shallower waters. Then, on February 19th, the Naval Research vessel *Mizar* with computerized under-water tracking equipment on board was added to Task Force 65 to keep an under-water eye on *Alvin* and *Aluminaut*. They could get to the bottom all right, and search—but they could not keep a record of where they had been. *Mizar* would do this for them.

From then until March 3rd, organized search of the two mile circle continued. Meanwhile, the Air Force teams ashore were still hunting and their search area was still spreading. It spread north and east and upwards into steep mountains where helicopters had to be brought in to lift the searchers up on to the high ground. It spread downwards to the bottoms of over 800 abandoned mine shafts—but there was no bomb. Then, on March 3rd, the whole situation was reviewed and the main effort was switched to the naval search, while 4,879 barrels of soil from the fields—the precious topsoil containing radio-active particles—were consigned to the Atomic Energy Commission site in South Carolina for burial.

At sea, contacts were found, numbered, investigated and—eliminated. Even mysterious tracks on the bottom were found, followed and lost—until, on March 12th, *Alvin* was assigned to investigate 'Contact 261'. The investigation was highly success-ful—'Contact 261' was the missing bomb. *Alvin* found it covered like a shrouded body with its own parachute and lying wedged in a crevice 2,550 feet down on a submarine mountainside. It was on a 70-degree slope—a slope which led steeply down to a submarine gorge where the water was 4,000 feet deep. It was five and a half miles off shore. Plotted on the search chart, it was in the south-east corner of 'C3'.

Alvin's mechanical claw, left off while searching, was put back again and attempts were made to fix a special clamp round the bomb for lifting by the *Mizar*. All were unsuccessful, partly because the slope was too steep for *Alvin* to land and partly because of the billowing parachute. On the fourth attempt, on

March 24th, they managed to get several of the parachute lines well tangled up on a grapnel and *Mizar* commenced lifting it. It cleared the crevice and success was almost in sight—when the line parted and it fell to the bottom again.

The position, of course, had already been accurately fixed by *Mizar*. Deteriorating weather prevented re-location attempts being made that day, but on the next both *Alvin* and *Aluminaut* dived—but failed to find it. They found the track made by the bomb as it was being hoisted off the bottom but—no bomb. Six more days of searching and then, on April 2nd, *Alvin* spotted it again, only 120 yards away from its previous resting place— but 250 feet deeper. It had slid down the slope.

Alvin and *Aluminaut* took it in turns to watch that it did not get away again and next morning *Alvin* fixed an alarm clock to it. Two 'pingers' were secured to the parachute; a transducer was dropped near by—and *Mizar* commenced a round-the-clock listening in. They were not going to lose the bomb a second time, and they were not going to risk it taking a toboggan ride down the slope without their knowing.

Next day, a strange contraption called CURV arrived by air from Pasadena. It was a most unusual beast—a sort of under-water bloodhound retriever. On a leash 3,100 feet long it went down to the bottom, smelled out its prey, shot out its paw, tied up its quarry with rope and brought the lot back to its master. This peculiar monster weighed a ton, was 13 feet long, 6 feet high and 5 feet wide. The leash was a control cable by which signals were sent down to CURV and its own television signals monitored. Its nose was an electronic ear, one eye was an under-water television camera and the other a movie camera. Its paw was a sort of electronic claw which could, probably, all but tie up parcels—but its owner bore absolutely no resemblance to a bloodhound nor, in fact, to any other animal on earth. It was christened Cable-controlled Under-water Research Vehicle and was nicknamed CURV for short. (Plate 16*a*.)

On Friday April 1st, CURV was taken on board the USS *Petrel* at Cartagena and then joined the Task Force off Palomares. On the 4th, CURV went down on test to a depth of 2,900 feet and next day, guided by *Alvin*, was sent down to the

bomb at 2,800 feet and attached a line to the top of the parachute. The other end of this line was then secured to a buoy on
the surface, and the first stage in the recovery operation had
been successfully completed.

Then the wind started to increase and sea conditions
deteriorated. In the evening, after CURV had been brought
up, *Alvin* went down again to check up on the position of the
bomb and its parachute. An hour after submerging she reached
the bottom at the spot where the bomb had been resting when
the line was attached. It was nowhere to be seen. The lie of the
buoy indicated that it was still attached to something, and
everyone knew that that 'something' was nearly 3,000 feet
below. But had it broken adrift and the line just caught in a
jagged crevice? Just as near-panic was prevailing above, *Alvin*
reported that she had spotted the parachute again on the bottom
—but it was 300 feet west-south-west from its previous position
and 50 feet farther down the slope. A hurried check on their
detailed contour chart of the sea bed showed that if it continued
slipping westward it would go down to 3,600 feet, while if it
slid southward it could end up at the bottom of a chasm 4,200
feet deep. There was no time to be lost.

Petrel, with CURV aboard, moved 300 feet to the bomb's
new position and, despite the night and worsening sea conditions, CURV was preparing for a second dive, when another
crisis developed all too suddenly. *Alvin* had become tangled up
in the still billowing parachute and for almost fifteen minutes
hovered on the brink of disaster. Down there, half a mile
beneath the now turbulent sea, *Alvin*'s crew at last managed to
free their tiny craft from the enveloping 65-foot diameter
parachute and two hours later, long past midnight, she surfaced
safely to everyone's relief.

Just after 8 o'clock next morning, April 6th, CURV started
once more on her long descent and by 10 o'clock had succeeded
in tying another nylon rope to half a dozen of the parachute
shrouds. This second line was also secured to a floating buoy.
In the early hours of April 7th, CURV was sent down for the
third time to attach the final line but this time the biter was
herself bit. She, too, became entangled but more so than *Alvin*
had been. CURV had tied itself up in the parachute lines. All

attempts to get it free were unsuccessful and it was therefore decided to lift both bomb and CURV together.

The buoyed lines were taken aboard *Petrel* and at 7 o'clock she began the delicate and dangerous task of hoisting up from nearly 3,000 feet the one-ton CURV tangled up with a 2¼-ton hydrogen bomb and its gigantic parachute. All went well. By 8 o'clock the strange load was suspended 50 feet below the recovery vessel. Divers went down, cut CURV free from the parachute and then attached two lifting straps to the bomb itself. Forty-five minutes later it was all over. The 5,000-pound hydrogen bomb, dented but intact, was back in man's keeping. (Plate 16*b*.)

On that fateful day nearly three months earlier, ejected so unceremoniously from its burning cradle 30,500 feet above Palomares, it had floated down, borne by its grey-white billowing shroud, into the sea. Then on, down, to the submerged mountainside nearly 3,000 feet beneath the surface of the blue Mediterranean. Hunted, found, lost again, and then snared by a monster under-water ferret, it was at last returned to its keepers.

In those eighty days which had elapsed since January 17th, a task force involving seventeen ships and 3,400 men had searched the sea bed and recovered over 50 tons of aircraft wreckage. More than 300 objects had been picked up from the ocean floor—objects ranging from a 30-foot long wing section to secret devices no larger than matchboxes. That which was lost had been found. The finding had cost the United States 15,000,000 dollars.

The cost was great, but the achievement was even greater. One day man will, no doubt, grow up and acquire enough wisdom and understanding to enable him to live at peace with his fellow creatures. His ingenuity may then, perhaps, be directed into more worth while channels.

CONVERSION TABLES

These conversion tables have been compiled to cover only those ranges of measurements, distances and weights which are mentioned in the book.

No conversion table for miles/kilometres has been included because all distances expressed in miles are sea distances for which the nautical mile of 6,080 feet is used. The metric equivalent of 8,080 feet, which is the mean length of a minute of latitude, is however 1·853 kilometres. For comparison, the metric equivalent of the land or statute mile of 5,280 feet is 1·609 kilometres and the nautical mile is equivalent to 1·15 statute miles.

When converting the tonnages of ships it should be borne in mind that the tonnage given for a merchant ship is normally the gross tonnage which is the cubic capacity of the vessel expressed in tons of 100 cubic feet to the ton. This is, therefore, a measurement tonnage and not the weight of the ship. The tonnage given for a warship is normally the displacement tonnage, or weight of water displaced, and is, therefore, the weight of the vessel.

As, however, a metric tonne is equivalent to 2204·6 lbs. which is only about 1½ per cent less than a British ton of 2,240 lbs., conversion may not be thought necessary.

DISTANCES

Inches	Feet	Yards	Centimetres	Metres	Kilometres
1			2·54		
1½			3·81		
2			5·08		
2½			6·35		
3			7·62		
3½			8·89		
4			10·16		
4½			11·43		
5			12·70		
5½			13·97		
6	½		15·24		
6½			16·51		
7			17·78		
7½			19·05		
8			20·32		
8½			21·59		
9			22·86		
9½			24·13		
10			25·40		
10½			26·67		
11			27·94		
11½			29·21		
12	1		30·48		
	2		60·96		
	3		91·44		
	4			1·219	
	5			1·524	
	6			1·829	
	7			2·134	
	8			2·438	
	9			2·743	
	10			3·048	
	20			6·096	
	30			9·144	
	40			12·192	
	50			15·240	
	60			18·288	
	70			21·336	
	80			24·384	
	90			27·432	
	100			30·480	
	200			60·960	
	300	100		91·440	
	400			121·920	
	500			152·400	
	600	200		182·880	
	700			213·360	
	800			243·840	
	900	300		274·320	
	1,000			304·800	
	2,000			609·600	
	3,000	1,000		914·400	
	4,000				1·219
	5,000				1·524

Inches	Feet	Yards	Centimetres	Metres	Kilometres
	6,000	2,000			1·829
	7,000				2·134
	8,000				2·438
	9,000	3,000			2·743
	10,000				3·048
	20,000				6·096
	30,000	10,000			9·144
	40,000				12·192
	50,000				15·240
	60,000	20,000			18·288
	70,000				21·336
	80,000				24·384
	90,000	30,000			27·432
	100,000				30·480

WEIGHTS

Ounces	Lbs.	Cwts.	Tons	Grams	Kilograms	Metric Tonnes
1				28·4		
4	¼			113		
8	½			227		
12	¾			340		
16	1			454		
	2			907		
	3				1·361	
	4				1·814	
	5				2·268	
	6				2·722	
	7				3·175	
	8				3·629	
	9				4·082	
	10				4·536	
	20				9·072	
	28	¼			12·700	
	30				13·608	
	40				18·144	
	50				22·680	
	56	½			25·401	
	60				27·216	
	70				31·752	
	80				36·287	
	84	¾			38·101	
	90				40·823	
	100				45·359	
	112	1			50·802	
		2			101·6	
		3			152·4	
		4			203·2	
		5	¼		254·0	
		6			304·8	
		7			355·6	
		8			406·4	
		9			457·2	
		10	½		508	

CONVERSION TABLES

Ounces	Lbs.	Cwts.	Tons	Grams	Kilograms	Metric Tonnes
			1		1016	1·016
			2			2·032
			3			3·048
			4			4·064
			5			5·080
			6			6·096
			7			7·112
			8			8·128
			9			9·145
			10			10·161
			20			20·321
			30			30·481
			40			40·642
			50			50·803
			60			60·963
			70			71·124
			80			81·284
			90			91·445
			100			101·606
			200			203·21
			300			304·82
			400			406·42
			500			508·63
			600			609·64
			700			711·24
			800			812·85
			900			914·45
			1,000			1016·05
			2,000			2032·1
			3,000			3048·2
			4,000			4064·2
			5,000			5080·3
			6,000			6096·4
			7,000			7112·4
			8,000			8128·5
			9,000			9144·5
			10,000			10,160
			20,000			20,321
			30,000			30,481
			40,000			40,642
			50,000			50,802
			60,000			60,962
			70,000			71,123
			80,000			81,283
			90,000			91,444
			100,000			101,604

BIBLIOGRAPHY

A Handbook on Evolution.
  Gavin de Beer. London, 1958.
Blackwood's Magazine, September 1954. 'Operation Elba Isle'.
  Gerald Forsberg. Edinburgh, 1954
Civil Aircraft Accident: Report of Court of Inquiry into the Accidents to
  Comet G-ALYP on 10th January 1954 and
  Comet G-ALYY on 8th April 1954
  Ministry of Transport and Civil Aviation, London, 1955
Death of the Thresher.
  Norman Polmar. New York, 1964
Deep Diving and Submarine Operations.
  Robert H. Davis. 7th Edition, Chessington, 1962
Exploring the Secrets of the Sea.
  William J. Cromie. London, 1962
Gold From the Sea.
  J. R. W. Taylor. Sydney, 1942
Marine Salvage Operations.
  Edward M. Brady, Cambridge, Mass., U.S.A.
Niagara Gold.
  R. J. Dunn. Wellington, New Zealand, 1942
Seventy Fathoms Deep.
  David Scott. London
Sunken Treasure.
  Pierre de Latil and Jean Rivoire. London, 1962

BIBLIOGRAPHY

The Bombs of Palomares.
Tad Szulc. London, 1967

The Egypt's Gold.
David Scott. Harmondsworth.

The Institution of Engineers and Shipbuilders in Scotland:
Transactions, Volume 93, Paper No. 1122, 'Marine Salvage in Peace and War'.
T. McKenzie C.B., C.B.E. 28.11.49. Glasgow, 1950.

The Man Who Bought A Navy.
Gerald Bowman. London, 1964

Underwater Television as Applied to Operation Elba Isle.
G. G. MacNeice. Admiralty Research Laboratory, Teddington, 1954

United States Naval Institute Proceedings, June 1967. Contact 261.
Captain Lewis B. Melson, U.S. Naval Institute, Annapolis, Maryland, U.S.A.

Wrinkles in Practical Navigation.
S. T. S. Lecky, Master Mariner, Commander R.N.R., F.R.A.S., F.R.G.S. etc. 23rd Edition 1956. George Philip & Son Limited, London

INDEX

INDEX

Ocean Bottom Scanning Sonar, 182
Operation Elba Isle, 127–37, 139
Orts, F. Simo, 179, 182

Palomares, 174–86
Parma, Duke of, 57
Pearl fisheries, 4
Pepys, Samuel, 50
Pereira, Andres, 59–61
Petrel, USS, 184–6
Phips, William, 45–55
Philip, King of Spain, 56
Piccard, Auguste, 11, 161
Piccard, Jacques, 11, 14
Pinnacle, USS, 181, 182
Poireau, M. M. 102
Princess, 53
Prinzregent Luitpold, battleship, 89–91
Puerto Plata, 48–52
Puriri, 124
Pye underwater television, 146, 153

Quaglia, Giovanni, 99–112

Raffio, 103–5
Ramage, Rear Admiral, 160
Rostro, 98–103
Rosario, 19, 22
Rosyth, 78, 80, 84–5, 87–9, 91, 93
Royal Aircraft Establishment (RAE), 137–9, 146–7, 150, 156
Rysa Little, 73, 81, 93

Saddle Rock Refuelling Area, 176
Salvage Association, 97, 111, 113
Sandberg, Peter, 97, 111, 113
Santa Fé, 19
Scapa Flow, 23, 28, 72–94
Scorpion, USS, 166–73
Scyllias, 3
Sea Salvor, 129–137
Seine, 95–6, 103
Seydlitz, battle cruiser, 79, 85–8
Skylark, USS, 158–9

Smalls Lighthouse, 141, 147, 148, 150
Société Nouvelle des Pêcheries à Vapeur, 98, 111
SORIMA, 9, 10, 98, 103, 107, 113
Spring tides, 18, 146
SubSafe, 167, 168
Swilly, Lough, 62, 64
Swinburne, James, 97, 113

Taranga Island, 118
Task Force 65, 180–1, 183
Thresher, USS, 157–65, 167, 171
Thucydides, 3
Tinnevelly fishery, 4
Tobermory Bay, 56–61
Transits, 29
Transit sonar, 33
Trieste, 11–13, 161–4
Trieste II, 166, 172
Twyford, 144–56
Tyre, 3

Underwater house, 14
Union des Entreprises Sousmarines, 98
United Salvage Proprietary, 116
Ushant, 95, 104, 168

V.70, destroyer, 74–7, 79
Victor Mark 2 bomber, 32, 44, 141–56
Vityaz, 13
Von der Tann, battle cruiser, 89–91
von Reuter, Admiral, 73, 79

Wakeful, HMS, 131–4
Whangarei, 119, 120, 122–3, 124
Whirlwind, HMS, 134
Williams, J.P., 116, 119
Wrangler, HMS, 130–1

Xerxes, 3